TRAVERS - DADE
from KEITH LODER. 1978

500 Animals from A-Z

BY

Tibor Gergely

WITH TEXT BY

Joseph A Davis

Hamlyn

LONDON · NEW YORK · SYDNEY · TORONTO

INTRODUCTION

The five hundred animals in these pages may seem a great many; they are, but they represent only a very small fraction of the kinds of animals alive in the world today. If we count every kind of animal, from the gigantic blue whale to the tiny creatures that are visible only under a microscope, we will find that there are over a million kinds of animals. Less than four thousand of these are mammals like ourselves, about nine thousand are birds, about six thousand are reptiles or amphibians, and twenty thousand are fishes of one kind or another. All these animals have backbones. But there are about twenty times as many kinds of insects as there are of all the backboned animals put together. Now you have an idea of how many *kinds* of animals there are, but what about the number of *individual* animals? No one really knows how many individual animals there are, but one thing is certain—the insects far outnumber the animals with backbones.

Once there were very few people in the world and they lived by hunting animals. In those days man's hunting made very little difference in the world. New animals were born and took the place of those that were killed, and when a few people cut down a patch of forest or turned a grassy meadow into a farm field, only a few animals had to look elsewhere for homes. When a village grew in the wilderness, the animals simply stayed away from it. Today there are more than three billion people alive in the world—that's three thousand people for each kind of animal. When they hunt animals today, they kill huge numbers, more than can be replaced by new births. Farms, villages, towns, and great cities occupy more and more land, and their refuse pollutes the land and the waters. Forests are cut down to become new farms. Every day wild animals find less and less living space. Many kinds of animals no longer exist because man has destroyed them, and many animals shown on these pages will be killed off in the next few years unless man learns in time that he must share the world with them. Whales are killed for dog food, and leopards, for fur coats. Other animals are threatened unintentionally by chemicals, such as DDT, which are used to control insects. People still look upon the larger animals, such as wolves and elephants, as either enemies or competitors for living space, and because they do not see the importance of these animals, they shoot them.

But people can also help to save animals. The American bison was nearly extinct a hundred years ago, when a few men persuaded the government to set aside special land. To this refuge New York's Bronx Zoo shipped many of its large herd. The bison have multiplied and are no longer in danger of dying out. Whooping cranes are very carefully protected today, and their numbers are beginning to increase. New laws make it a crime to kill an alligator or to sell its

Published 1972 by
The Hamlyn Publishing Group Limited
LONDON · NEW YORK · SYDNEY · TORONTO
Hamlyn House, Feltham, Middlesex, England
by arrangement with American Heritage Press.

ISBN 0 600 33488 0
Printed in England by Cox & Wyman, Fakenham

skin. Today there is still a chance to save many other endangered species. As you grow up more kinds of animals will become scarce, but you will have a chance to help them. By the time you are an adult, some of the animals in this book will no longer exist, and others will be found only in zoos. How many more disappear after that will depend on how much you and your neighbours value the strange and beautiful creatures that share your world.

A Note from Tibor Gergely

When we hear the word "animal", most of us think first of mammals such as the lion or the bear or the mouse. But "animal" also means other creatures—birds or fishes or insects or reptiles. In the pages that follow, you will recognize many animals that you have already heard about or seen in a zoo, on a holiday trip, or even in your back garden; others will be creatures you are meeting for the first time. My friend Johnny, eight years old, heard me mentioning three animals—the binturong, the kea, and the tuatara—and wanted to know what they were and what they looked like. First he had to consult the dictionary, then he had to look in a book on mammals to find out about the binturon, a book on birds for the kea, and a book on reptiles for the tuatara. The alphabetical arrangement of the animals assembled here will make it easier for Johnny (and for you) to find this information in one book.

It was not possible within these pages to do more than introduce briefly any one kind of animal. From among the tens of thousands of different kinds of animals in the world today, we selected the more than five hundred you will see here because they were among the most interesting or beautiful or typical. I hope you will find that each of them is worth knowing better.

This book can give you only a glimpse of them. After you have met these animals, perhaps you will want to look in your school or public library for other books that deal with fewer animals, but tell you more about each.

Many of these creatures have several names. The index in the back of this book lists the most familiar of their various names and tells you where to find the animals' pictures and descriptions. For instance, if you look for the *marabou*, the index will tell you to see the *adjutant*, which is its other popular name. If you are interested in *antelope*, the index will show you how many different kinds of antelope you can find.

Aardvark 4 ft. *(1·2 m.)*

The AARDVARK has a snout like a pig's and strong claws. It uses them to open the hard nests of ants and termites, which it can then catch with its long, sticky tongue.

Abalone 10 in. *(25·4 cm.)*

ABALONES have only one shell. They protect themselves by holding tight to rocks.

Adder, Puff $3\frac{1}{2}$ ft. *(1·1 m.)*

The PUFF ADDER is a stout-bodied venomous snake of Africa. It gets its name from its loud hissing and puffing.

Adjutant 5 ft. *(1·5 m.)*

ADJUTANTS are storks that live by scavenging, as vultures do.

Agouti 1 ft. 4 in. *(40·5 cm.)*

AGOUTIS are cousins of guinea pigs and porcupines. Of the many kinds that exist, most are the same shade of red or grey.

Albatross

4 ft. *(1·2 m.)* wingspan over 11 ft. *(3·3 m.)*

ALBATROSSES are big sea birds that soar far out to sea on air currents. They have wingspreads up to 11 ft. *(3·3 m.)*—the greatest of any bird.

Alligator 16 ft. *(4·8 m.)*

The ALLIGATOR is not nearly so ferocious or dangerous as the crocodile. The "gator holes" that it digs in time of drought provide water for the other creatures of the American everglades. Poachers may soon make it extinct.

Anaconda 25 ft. *(7·6 m.)*

The ANACONDA is one of the longest snakes in the world, growing to a length of 20 ft. *(6 m.)* —possibly more than 30 ft. *(9 m.)*. It lives near water and is a good swimmer. It is not venomous.

Angelfish 2 ft. *(60·9 cm.)*

ANGELFISH have flattened bodies with large fins above and below. Most kinds are very colourful.

Anglerfish 6 in. *(15·2 cm.)*

ANGLERFISH catch other fish by using a built-in fishing rod. When a small fish comes near the "bait," the angler swallows its prey.

Anhinga 3 ft. *(91·4 cm.)*

The ANHINGA'S long neck has earned it the name "snakebird". It eats fishes and other water creatures.

Anole 7 in. *(17·8 cm.)*

ANOLES are small lizards often sold in pet shops as chameleons. They change colour from green to brown.

Ant

ANTS are found all over the world, and some kinds build their nests in the form of ANTHILLS. All ants have very narrow waists.

Anteater 7 ft. *(2·1 m.)*

ANTEATERS have no teeth, but their long sticky tongues are ideal for catching ants and termites. The GIANT ANTEATER walks on its knuckles to protect the sharpness of its claws. Although not closely related to the aardvark, it eats ants in much the same way.

Antelope 6 ft. *(1·8 m.)*

ANTELOPE come in all sizes and shapes, from the eland down to the little royal antelope. In some kinds, such as the SABLE ANTELOPE shown here, both male and female have horns, while in other kinds, such as the kudu, only the male has them. Antelope horns take many shapes; see how many you can find in this book.

Aoudad 5 ft. *(1·5 m.)*

The AOUDAD is unusual among wild sheep because of its long shaggy beard.

Archerfish 8 in. *(20·3 cm.)*

The ARCHERFISH knocks down the insects it eats by squirting water from its mouth like a living water pistol.

Armadillo 5 ft. *(1·5 m.)*

ARMADILLOS carry in their skin their own armour, which is made of bony plates covered with a layer of horn. The three-banded armadillo shown rolled up has shields on its head and tail that fit together. The GIANT ARMADILLO often weighs over 100 lb. *(45 kgm.)*.

Asparagus Beetle $\frac{3}{10}$ in. *(7·6 mm.)*

As you might guess from its name, the ASPARAGUS BEETLE eats asparagus plants.

Atlas Moth over 1 ft. *(30·5 cm)* wingspan

The ATLAS MOTH is one of the world's biggest moths, with a wingspan of 10 in. *(25 cm.)*

Auk, Razor-billed 1 ft. 4 in. *(40·5 cm.)*

The RAZOR-BILLED AUK is the Northern Hemisphere's version of its distant relative the penguin. It is a fine swimmer and diver and it eats fishes, shrimp, and other small sea creatures.

Aye-aye 1 ft. 4 in. *(40·5 cm.)*
The AYE-AYE of Madagascar uses its long thin third finger to dig out insects that bore in wood and to comb its fur. You'd never guess that the aye-aye is a cousin of the monkeys and lemurs.

Babirusa 3 ft. *(91·4 cm.)*
The BABIRUSA is a wild pig; the male has tusks that grow up through the roof of its mouth and snout.

Baboon $2\frac{1}{2}$ ft. *(76·2 cm.)*
BABOONS are big monkeys with long, doglike muzzles. All of them, like this HAMADRYAS BABOON, live on the ground.

Badger, Eurasian 2 ft. 4 in. *(71·1 cm.)*
The EURASIAN BADGER lives in family groups in a series of burrows called a set.

Barbary Ape 1 ft. 10 in. *(55·8 cm.)*
The BARBARY APE is not an ape at all, but a monkey that lives in North Africa and on Gibraltar. A legend says that British rule of Gibraltar will end when the monkeys leave, so the British take very good care of them.

Barnacle $\frac{1}{2}$ to 2 in. *(12·7 to 50·8 mm.)*
BARNACLES swim free when they are young and then attach themselves permanently to large objects—rocks, ships, and even whales.

Barracuda, Great
5 to 10 ft. *(1·5 to 3 m.)*
The GREAT BARRACUDA grows to a length of 6 ft. *(1·8 m.)* and is one of the most dangerous fishes in the ocean.

Bass, Largemouth $1\frac{1}{2}$ ft. *(45·7 cm.)*
LARGEMOUTH BASS will eat almost any small water creatures, from worms to small fishes. Water temperature affects their growth; in the southern United States they grow to a weight of 10 lb. *(4 kgm.)* or more, but in the North they are less than half as big.

Bat $4\frac{1}{2}$ in. *(11·4 cm.)*, wingspan 1 ft. *(30·5 cm.)*

BATS are the only mammals that can really fly. Their wings are actually very big hands with a thin web of skin between the fingers. Most kinds of bats, like the BIG BROWN BAT shown here, catch and eat insects in the air; others feed on fruits, nectar, small animals, and even blood.

Bear, Alaskan Brown

9 to 10 ft. *(2·7 to 3 m.)*

The ALASKAN BROWN BEAR is the world's largest bear—it weighs as much as ten full-grown men. Bears eat all sorts of things, from meat to plants. They do not really hibernate, but many of them sleep soundly for weeks at a time in winter.

Beaver $3\frac{1}{2}$ ft. *(1·1 m.)*

BEAVERS are the second-largest rodents in the world. They live in ponds, which they sometimes make by damming a stream with sticks and mud. Beavers cut down trees, eat the inner bark, and then use the wood for building.

Bee (Honeybee) $\frac{1}{2}$ in. *(12·7 mm.)*

The HONEYBEE has been kept by man for some forty centuries. In addition to providing honey, it helps many plants to fruit and flower by carrying pollen from one plant to others like it.

Beetle, Burying $1\frac{1}{4}$ in. *(31·7 mm.)*

BURYING BEETLES actually bury small dead animals. Fly maggots grow in the carcasses, and the beetles' young feed on the maggots.

Bighorn Sheep 5 ft. *(1·5 m.)*

The male BIGHORN SHEEP has magnificent curled horns. When two males battle, the crash of their horns resounds through the mountains.

Big Brown Bat

Beaver

Honeybee

Bighorn Sheep

Burying Beetle

Alaskan Brown Bear (Kodiak)

Binturong 3 ft. *(91·4 cm.)*

The BINTURONG, a big civet that lives in trees, has a long bushy tail that can grasp branches. It eats mostly fruit and it smells something like peanut butter.

Bird of Paradise 1 ft. 2 in. *(35·5 cm.)*

All female BIRDS OF PARADISE look very much alike, but the males of each species have distinctive bright colours and oddly shaped plumes.

Bison, American 10 ft. *(3 m.)*

The AMERICAN BISON (sometimes called the buffalo) was once found by the millions in North America, but was almost wiped out by greedy and thoughtless hunters. It has been carefully protected since then, and now there are a great many in North American national parks.

Bittern, American

2 ft. 10 in. *(86·3 cm.)*

When the AMERICAN BITTERN is threatened, it points its bill straight up and stands very still. In that position the markings on its throat and body make it look like the tall reeds in which it lives.

Black Widow Spider

2 in. *(50·8 mm.)* overall

The BLACK WIDOW SPIDER, like many other kinds of spiders, has a venomous bite, but it bites only in self-defence.

Bluebird 7 in. *(17·7 cm.)*
The BLUEBIRD likes to sit on a wire fence or in a bush to watch for insects to eat.

Boa Constrictor 15 ft. *(4·5 m.)*
The BOA CONSTRICTOR is an excellent climber and spends considerable time in trees.

Boar, Wild up to 5 ft. *(1·5 m.)*
The WILD BOAR is the ancestor of our domestic pigs. Although it fights fiercely when threatened, it is usually peaceful. Like other kinds of pigs, it eats almost anything.

Bobcat 2 ft. 8 in. *(81·2 cm.)*
The BOBCAT is named after its short, "bobbed" tail. Its ear tufts are shorter than those of its close relative the lynx.

Bobolink 8 in. *(20·3 cm.)*
The BOBOLINK can be heard singing its bubbling song far above the fields where it lives.

Bongo $3\frac{1}{2}$ ft. *(1·1 m.)* at the shoulders
The BONGO is a large antelope—one of the most beautiful. Unlike most other kinds of antelope, it lives in forests rather than in open, grassy plains.

Bonito 3 ft. *(91·4 cm.)*
The BONITO is a cousin of the tuna; it is smaller and less prized as food.

Boa Constrictor
Bobcat (Wildcat)
Wild Boar
Bluebird
Bongo
Bobolink

Bowerbird 1 ft. 1 in. *(33 cm.)*

BOWERBIRD males build bowers, places where they court the females. The SATIN BOWERBIRD makes an avenue edged with upright twigs.

Box Turtle 5 to 6 in. *(12 to 15·2 cm.)*

The lower shell of BOX TURTLES is hinged and can be pulled up like a trap door after the turtle has pulled in its head.

Buffalo, Cape 8 to 9 ft. *(2·4 to 2·7 m.)*

BUFFALOES are wild cattle of Africa and Asia, although the name is sometimes wrongly used for the bison. The CAPE BUFFALO can weigh as much as 1 ton *(1 tonne)*.

Bullfinch 6 in. *(15·2 cm.)*

Because of its ability to learn new songs, the BULLFINCH is often kept as a pet.

Bullfrog 6 in. *(15·2 cm.)*

The BULLFROG is the largest frog in North America: its body may grow to a length of 8 in. *(20 cm.)*.

Bumblebee 1 in. *(2·5 cm.)*

BUMBLEBEES are big, hairy bees that make their nests underground. Their wings make a very loud buzzing sound when they fly.

Bunting, Painted 5¼ in. *(13·3 cm.)*

The PAINTED BUNTING is one of the most brightly coloured of North American birds. It is often found along the overgrown edges of roads.

Bush Baby 1 ft. 8 in. *(50·8 cm.)*

BUSH BABIES, or galagos, are agile cousins of the pottos. Their big eyes help them see at night when they leap among the branches of trees.

Bushmaster 12 ft. *(3·6 m.)*

The BUSHMASTER, which can grow to a length of 11 ft. *(3.3 m.)*, is the longest venomous snake of the New World. Unlike its cousins the rattlesnakes, it does not bear living young but lays eggs.

Bustard 4½ ft. *(1·3 m.)*

BUSTARDS are large birds that eat mainly plants and insects. There are about two dozen kinds, and all are swift runners.

Butterfly

6/10 in. to 2 in. *(15·2 mm. to 50·8 mm.)* wingspan

BUTTERFLIES differ from moths in having knobs on their antennae and in being active in the daytime. They have big wings covered with tiny overlapping scales, usually of bright colours. Butterflies start life as caterpillars; then, instead of making cocoons, most butterfly caterpillars form chrysalids before becoming adults. Many butterflies are named for their colour, like the BLUE and the SULPHUR, while others, like the CABBAGE WHITE, are also named for the plant on which they feed.

Buzzard 2 ft. 5 in. *(73·6 cm.)*

The name "BUZZARD" means different things in different parts of the world. In Europe buzzards are broad-winged hawks, but in America the name is often wrongly applied to the TURKEY VULTURE shown here.

Cacomistle $2\frac{1}{2}$ ft. *(76·2 cm.)*

The CACOMISTLE is sometimes called ring-tailed cat, but it is actually related closely to the raccoon.

Caiman 6 ft. *(1·8 m.)*

CAIMANS are tropical cousins of the alligators. They never grow as large as alligators, but their dispositions are much more unpleasant.

Camel, Arabian

8 ft. *(2·4 m.)* at the shoulders

The ARABIAN CAMEL, or dromedary, has a single hump. For centuries it has been used as a beast of burden in the desert because it can go without water for several days at a time.

Canada Goose 3 ft. 4 in. *(1 m.)*

The CANADA GOOSE is one of the New World's most familiar water birds. Families of Canada geese stay together through their annual migration.

Canary 4 in. *(10 cm.)*

The CANARY originally came from the Canary Islands and was named after them.

Canvasback 2 ft. *(60·9 cm.)*

The CANVASBACK is a large duck. The female quacks and the male makes a grunting sound.

Capuchin Monkey 1 ft. 5 in. *(43·1 cm.)*

CAPUCHIN MONKEYS are common in South America. They are sometimes called ring-tailed monkeys because they often carry their tails rolled into a tight coil.

Capybara 4 ft. *(1·2 m.)*

The CAPYBARA is the largest of all rodents, sometimes weighing 100 lb. *(45 kgm.)*. It likes to swim and often escapes its enemies by taking to the water.

Cardinal 8 in. *(20·3 cm.)*

The CARDINAL uses its heavy bill to crack open the seeds it eats.

Caribou 6½ ft. *(1·9 m.)*

The CARIBOU, like its domesticated descendant the reindeer, is unusual among deer because the female, as well as the male, has antlers.

Carp up to 3 ft. *(91·4 cm.)*

The CARP is one of the few kinds of fish that can survive in badly polluted waters.

Cassowary 5 ft. 5 in. *(1·6 m.)*

CASSOWARIES are large birds with wings so small that they cannot fly and odd feathers that look like shaggy hair.

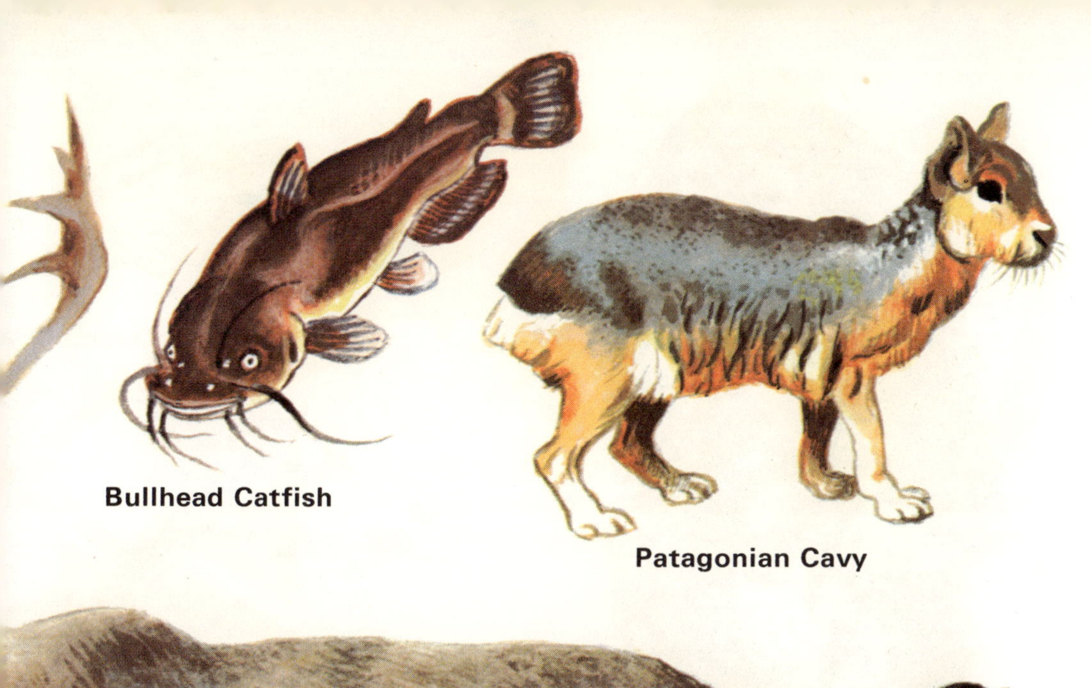

Bullhead Catfish

Patagonian Cavy

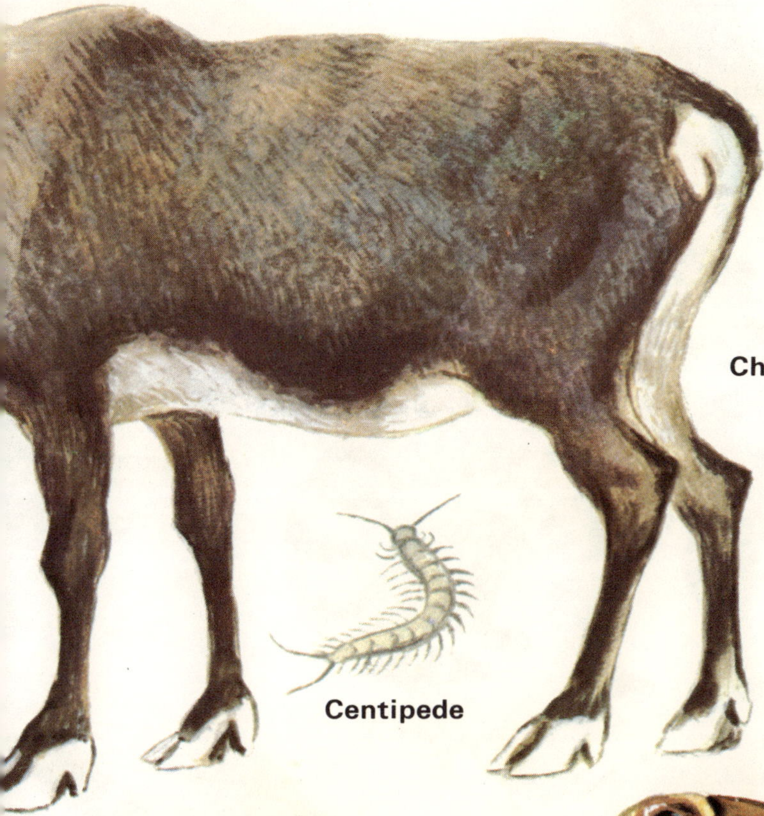

Chickadee

Centipede

Cecropia Moth

Chameleon

Cheetah

Catfish 1 ft. 3 in. *(38·1 cm.)*

Catfish have long, fleshy "whiskers" that are very sensitive to touch. Most kinds like muddy stream bottoms.

Cavy, Patagonian 2 ft. 4 in. *(70·1 cm.)*

The Patagonian Cavy lives in burrows and can run very fast; it can easily jump a fence of 4 ft. *(1·25 m.)*.

Cecropia Moth

$5\frac{1}{2}$ in. *(13·9 cm.)* wingspan

The Cecropia Moth is one of the largest of New World moths. Males find females by scent, which they can detect over great distances.

Centipede 1 to 2 in. *(25·4 to 50·8 mm.)*

Centipedes have poison fangs and eat other small creatures.

Chameleon 8 to 12 in. *(20·3 to 30·4 cm.)*

Chameleons are lizards that can change their colour. They shoot out their long, sticky tongues, which can extend the entire length of their bodies, to catch insects.

Cheetah 6 ft. 10 in. *(2·1 m.)*

The Cheetah can run faster than any other animal, but even its speed cannot protect it from hunters, who may soon make it extinct.

Chickadee $5\frac{1}{2}$ in. *(13·9 cm.)*

The Chickadee is an active little bird that eats insects in summer, but will come to a bird feeder in winter to eat seeds and suet.

Chimpanzee 4 ft. *(1·2 m.)*

The CHIMPANZEE is more like man than any other animal. In zoos and laboratories it has long been known for its cleverness, and lately scientists watching the chimpanzee in its native tropical rain forests have found that it is very bright at home too.

Chinchilla 1 ft. *(30·4 cm.)*

The CHINCHILLA has the softest, thickest fur known.

Chipmunk, Eastern 10 in. *(25·4 cm.)*

The EASTERN CHIPMUNK is a small striped squirrel that spends most of its time on the ground. It stores nuts and seeds in its burrow and wakes up from time to time in the winter to eat them.

Cicada $1\frac{8}{10}$ in. *(45 mm.)*

CICADAS fill the summer air with their whirring songs. The young of some kinds of cicadas take as long as fifteen years or more to become adults.

Civet, Oriental $2\frac{1}{2}$ ft. *(76·2 cm.)*

The ORIENTAL CIVET has scent glands that produce a musk used to make perfume.

Clam, Giant

1 to 5 ft. *(30·4 cm. to 1·5 m.)* across

The GIANT CLAM grows to a length of 5 ft. *(1·5 m.)* and can weigh as much as 500 lb. *(225 kgm.)*.

Click Beetle $1\frac{1}{4}$ in. *(31·7 mm.)*

If you place a CLICK BEETLE on its back it snaps its body upward with a clicking sound.

Coatimundi 2 ft. *(60·9 cm.)*

The COATIMUNDI, a long-nosed cousin of the raccoon, lives in troops that roam about eating all kinds of things, from fruit to small animals.

Eastern Chipmunk

Chinchilla

Chimpanzee

Annual Cicada

Oriental Civet

Giant Clam

Click Beetle

Coatimundi

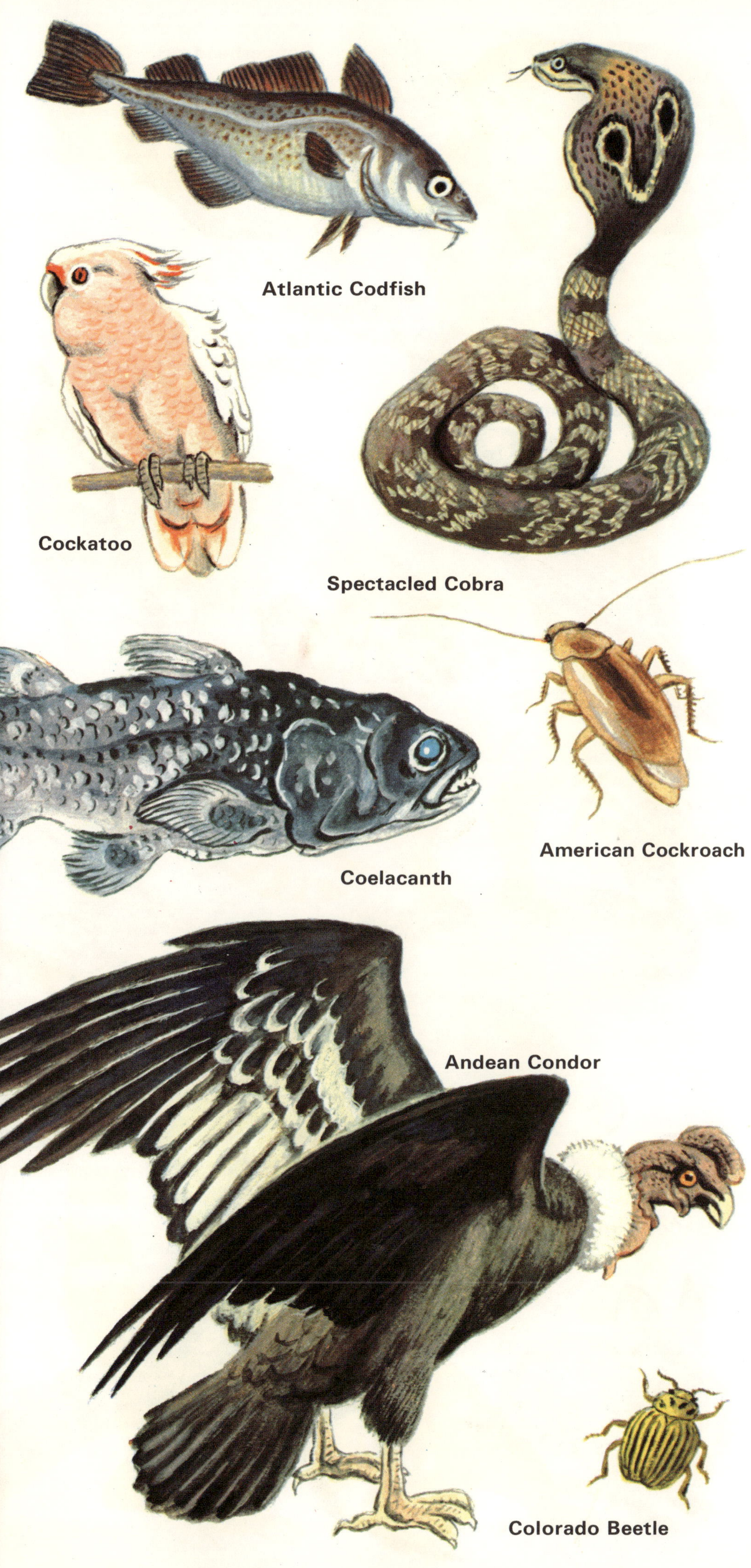

Atlantic Codfish

Cockatoo

Spectacled Cobra

Coelacanth

American Cockroach

Andean Condor

Colorado Beetle

Cobra 6 ft. *(1·8 m.)*

COBRAS spread the ribs in their neck region to form a hood when they are excited, but most of the time their necks are slim like those of other snakes. The eyeglass-shaped markings of the SPECTACLED COBRA show only when the hood is spread.

Cockatoo 1 ft. 3 in. *(38·1 cm.)*

The COCKATOO is a member of the parrot family. It has a strong beak, which it uses to crack open hard seeds.

Cockroach, American

1½ in. *(38·1 mm.)*

The AMERICAN COCKROACH is not a native of America; it was brought from Africa on slave ships.

Codfish, Atlantic

2 to 3 ft. *(60·9 to 91·4 cm.)*

The ATLANTIC CODFISH is one of the most important food fishes in the world.

Coelacanth 4 ft. *(1·2 m.)*

Scientists once believed that COELACANTHS, which were in the seas when dinosaurs were alive, had become extinct millions of years ago. In 1938, however, some fishermen caught one off the coast of Africa.

Colorado Beetle $\frac{4}{10}$ in. *(10 mm.)*

The COLORADO BEETLE, once a harmless insect, learned to like the taste of potato plants and is now a serious pest in both America and Europe.

Condor, Andean

4 ft. 4 in. *(1·3 m.)*, wingspan 9 ft. *(2·7 m.)*

The ANDEAN CONDOR is one of the largest of birds that fly. It has a wingspan of over 9 ft. *(2·7 m.)*.

Coot 1 ft. 4 in. *(39·6 cm.)*

The COOT swims like a duck. It is very slow getting into the air and seems to run on the water before it can take off.

Copperhead $2\frac{1}{2}$ to 4 ft. *(76·2 cm. to 1·2 m.)*

The American COPPERHEAD is related to the rattlesnakes, but its bite is somewhat less dangerous.

Coral Snake 3 ft. *(91·4 cm.)*

The CORAL SNAKE is as venomous as it is beautiful. It is docile and rarely strikes, but when it does, its bite is very dangerous.

Cormorant, Double-crested 3 ft. *(91·4 cm.)*

The DOUBLE-CRESTED CORMORANT can fly underwater to catch the fish it eats.

Cottontail Rabbit 1 ft. 4 in. *(39·6 cm.)*

When the COTTONTAIL RABBIT runs, the white underside of its tail is very easy to see; but when it stops, only the brown top of the tail is visible.

Coyote 4 ft. *(1·2 m.)*

The COYOTE is one of the few kinds of animals that have become more numerous and increased their ranges since man appeared on the scene.

Crab 6 in. *(15·2 cm.)* across
If a CRAB loses a claw in a fight, it can grow a new one.

Crane, Crowned 3 ft. 2 in. *(96·5 cm.)*
The CROWNED CRANE, like other cranes, courts its mate with a wild, leaping dance.

Cricket 1 in. *(25·4 mm.)*
The ears of CRICKETS are located on their front legs.

Crocodile, Nile 16 ft. *(4·8 m.)*
The fierce NILE CROCOCILE is said to let the small crocodile bird walk into its open mouth to pick out parasites.

Crow 1 ft. 9 in. *(53·3 cm.)*
CROWS are among the smartest of birds. Not only do they take responsibility for other members of the crow community, but in captivity they readily learn to imitate human speech.

Cuckoo, European 1 ft. 1 in. *(33 cm.)*
The EUROPEAN CUCKOO'S call is familiar to everyone who has heard a cuckoo clock. The cuckoo does not build a nest, but lays its eggs in the nests of other birds which then raise its young.

Curlew, Long-billed 2 ft. *(60·9 cm.)*
The LONG-BILLED CURLEW probes in the sand with its curved bill to find worms and other small creatures to eat.

Cuscus 2 ft. *(60·9 cm.)*
The CUSCUS can grasp branches with its tail, like an opossum. Naturally enough, it lives in trees.

Daddy Longlegs

$\frac{1}{4}$ in. *(6 mm.)*, legs 2 in. *(50·8 mm.)*

DADDY LONGLEGS are really flies, not spiders, so they don't make webs. But they can and do eat other insects.

Damselfly $1\frac{3}{10}$ in. *(33 mm.)*

Dragonfly 2 in. *(50·8 mm.)*

DAMSELFLIES can be told from their close relatives, DRAGONFLIES, by their thinner bodies. Damselflies at rest hold their wings with the edges up and down, while dragonflies hold their wings flat. Both catch small insects in flight.

Deer, White-tailed $5\frac{1}{2}$ ft. *(1·6 m.)*

WHITE-TAILED DEER are more numerous in America today than when Columbus discovered the New World, because many of the original forests have been replaced by grazing land.

Dingo 3 ft. *(91·4 cm.)*

The DINGO was taken to Australia by the men who first arrived there. Some dingos ran away and became wild, and their descendants have been wild ever since.

Dolphin, Common 8 ft. *(2·4 m.)*

The COMMON DOLPHIN is an air-breathing mammal, a cousin of the whales. It is playful and intelligent.

Dormouse, Common European

$2\frac{3}{4}$ in. *(69·8 mm.)*

The COMMON EUROPEAN DORMOUSE was eaten by the ancient Romans as a delicacy. Today, however, the dormouse is safe from gourmets.

Dog, Cape Hunting

3 ft. 4 in. *(99 cm.)*

CAPE HUNTING DOGS have always been wild. They hunt in packs and make odd squeaking sounds instead of barking or howling.

Dory 2 ft. *(60·9 cm.)*

A DORY is an ocean fish; some species are long and narrow, much like the small fishing boat that is also called a dory.

Dove, Mourning 1 ft. *(30·4 cm.)*

The MOURNING DOVE is the only bird that lives in all forty-nine of the continental United States.

Dugong 9 ft. *(2·7 m.)*

DUGONGS often "tread water" and float upright; because from a distance they look almost human, they may be the mermaids that sailors claim to have seen.

Duiker 2½ ft. *(76·2 cm.)*

DUIKERS are small antelope that live in the forests of Africa. The MAXWELL'S DUIKER is one of the smaller kinds, not much larger than a jack rabbit.

Eagle, Bald 3 ft. *(91·4 cm.)*

The BALD EAGLE is the official symbol of the United States. The main food of the eagle is fish, and because many fish are tainted by DDT, the eagle is being poisoned into extinction.

Earthworm

1 to 4 in. *(25·4 mm to 10·1 cm.)*

EARTHWORMS help the soil by mixing it as they move and by leaving little tunnels that let in air and rainwater.

Earwig $\frac{6}{10}$ in. *(15·2 mm.)*

EARWIGS are unusual insects with big pincers on their hind ends. Some kinds eat other insects, and many kinds are scavengers.

Echidna, Australian $1\frac{1}{2}$ ft. *(45·7 cm.)*

The AUSTRALIAN ECHIDNA, or spiny anteater, is a relative of the platypus. The female lays one egg, which she carries in a pouch on her belly.

Eel, Electric 5 ft. *(1·5 m.)*

The ELECTRIC EEL actually makes an electric shock that can be dangerous even to a large animal.

Eft, Red $2\frac{1}{2}$ in. *(63·5 cm.)*

The RED EFT is a newt in its land stage; it spends the first and last parts of its life in the water.

Egret, American 3 ft. 4 in. *(1 m.)*

AMERICAN EGRETS were once greatly endangered because they were killed for their plumes, which women wore in their hats. Strict laws were passed, and now egrets are common again.

Eider 2 ft. *(60·9 cm.)*

The female EIDER lines her nest with downy feathers that she pulls from her breast. After the ducklings have left the nest, people collect the feathers, called eiderdown, and use them to fill pillows and quilts.

Eland

10 ft. *(3 m.)*, 6 ft. *(1·8 m.)* at the shoulders

The ELAND is the largest of the antelope, although it looks more like a cow than its graceful nearest of kin.

Elephant, African 12 ft. *(3·6 m.)* tall

The AFRICAN ELEPHANT is the largest land animal in the world. A full-grown elephant has no natural enemies except man.

Elephant Seal 20 ft. *(6 m.)*
The male ELEPHANT SEAL has a bulbous nose that it puffs up with air to make a wide variety of puffs, sighs, snorts, and snores.

Emu 6 ft. 3 in. *(1·9 m.)*
The EMU is the second-largest bird in the world. The male emu sits on the eggs, and after they hatch, he takes care of the chicks.

Ermine 1 ft. 3 in. *(38·1 cm.)*
The ERMINE is a kind of weasel. In the northern parts of its range, the ermine turns white in winter and brown in summer.

Falcon, Peregrine 1½ ft. *(45·7 cm.)*
The PEREGRINE FALCON, when diving, can move as fast as 175 m.p.h. *(282 km.p.h.)*. Like the bald eagle, it is greatly endangered by the use of DDT.

Fennec 1 ft. 4 in. *(39·6 cm.)*
The FENNEC is a small fox with very large ears. It lives in the desert.

Fiddler Crab 2 in. *(50 mm.)* across
The male FIDDLER CRAB has one very large claw, which is used to signal females.

Finch, Purple 5½ in. *(13·9 cm.)*
The PURPLE FINCH usually nests high in evergreen trees. Like other finches, it eats seeds.

Firefly ½ in. *(12·7 mm.)*
Different kinds of FIREFLIES tell each other apart by the timing of their flashes of light.

Flamingo 4 ft. 2 in. *(1·2 m.)*
FLAMINGOES have strainers in their beaks that separate the diatoms, (almost microscopic algae) from the water in which they grow. Then the flamingoes swallow the diatoms.

Flea $\frac{1}{10}$ in. *(2·5 mm.)*
FLEAS live by sucking small amounts of blood from birds and mammals. There are about two hundred kinds of fleas.

Flounder $2\frac{1}{2}$ ft. *(76·2 cm.)*
Baby FLOUNDERS look like other young fish, but as they grow, one eye moves to the other side of the head and the flounders swim with that side upward.

Fly (Housefly) $\frac{3}{10}$ in. *(7·6 cm.)*
The HOUSEFLY is found all over the world and is one of man's worst pests.

Flycatcher, Crested 9 in. *(22·8 cm.)*
CRESTED FLYCATCHERS will attack larger birds that enter their nesting territory.

Flying Fish 1 ft. *(30·4 cm.)*
The big fins of FLYING FISH enable them to glide through the air for short distances.

Flying Fox 1 ft. 4 in. *(39·6 cm.)*
The FLYING FOX is really a bat. It can have a wingspan of almost 5 ft. *(1·5 m.)*.

Flying Squirrel 10 in. *(25·4 cm.)*
FLYING SQUIRRELS are the only squirrels that sleep all day and come out at night.

Fox, Red 3 ft. *(91·4 cm.)*
The RED FOX is one of the cleverest of animals when it comes to escaping from hunters.

Frigate Bird
3 ft. 4 in. *(1 m.)*, wingspan 7 ft. *(2·1 m.)*
At mating time the male FRIGATE BIRD puffs up its large throat sac to attract females.

Frog 1 in. *(25·4 mm.)* to $2\frac{1}{2}$ ft. *(76·2 cm.)*
FROGS come in many sizes, from the giant GOLIATH FROG of Africa to kinds even smaller than the American SPRING PEEPER.

Galápagos Tortoise

25 ft. *(7·6 m.)* over carapace

GALÁPAGOS TORTOISES are found only in the Galápagos Islands. They are the biggest tortoises in the world, and some kinds weigh 500 lb. *(225 kgm.)*.

Gallinule, Florida 1 ft. 2 in. *(35·5 cm.)*

The FLORIDA GALLINULE lives in marshes and swims as well as a duck.

Gannet 3 ft. 4 in. *(1 m.)*

The GANNET makes its nest on rocky ledges in high sea cliffs. It can dive as deep as 50 ft. *(15 m.)*. below the water to catch small fish.

Garter Snake

$1\frac{1}{2}$ to $3\frac{1}{2}$ in. *(38·1 to 88·9 mm.)*

GARTER SNAKES are among the commonest snakes in North America. They eat earthworms, insects, and sometimes small frogs.

Gavial 23 ft. *(7 m.)*

The GAVIAL has a long, thin snout that helps it catch fish.

Gazelle $3\frac{1}{2}$ ft. *(1·1 m.)*

GAZELLES are graceful and usually rather small antelope. The DORCAS GAZELLE stands about 2 ft. *(60 cm.)* high at the shoulders.

Gecko 4 to 5 in. *(10·1 to 12·7 cm.)*

GECKOS are able to climb smooth surfaces because their finger pads are lined with tiny hooks. Most kinds of geckos are active only at night.

Genet 1 ft. 8 in. *(50·5 cm.)*

Although the GENET is a member of the civet family, it can retract its claws like a cat.

Gerbil, Naked-soled 5 in. *(12·7 cm.)*

The NAKED-SOLED GERBIL lives in underground burrows during the day and comes out at night to find its food.

Gerenuk 5 ft. *(1·5 m.)*

The GERENUK, a kind of gazelle, can stand on its long hind legs and with its long neck reach leaves too high for other antelope to eat.

Gibbon 2 ft. *(60·9 cm.)*

GIBBONS look like monkeys but are actually apes. They use their long arms to swing through the trees like acrobats.

Gila Monster 2 ft. *(60·9 cm.)*

The GILA MONSTER is one of the only two poisonous lizards in the world.

Giraffe 19 ft. *(5·7 m.)*
The GIRAFFE'S long neck enables it to reach high into trees and feed on the leaves. In spite of its length, the neck has only seven bones, like your neck.

Gnat $\frac{1}{10}$ in. *(2·5 mm.)*
GNATS are very small flies that are most common in northern regions. Their bites are quite painful for such tiny creatures.

Gnatcatcher, Blue-grey 5 in. *(12·7 cm.)*
The BLUE-GREY GNATCATCHER is an American cousin of the Old World warblers. Constantly active, it can catch insects in flight.

Gnu 8 ft. *(2·4 m.)*
The GNU snorts and jumps around when approached. Herds of gnus (or wildebeests, as they are also called) often travel with zebra herds.

Goldfish 3 in. *(76 mm.)*
GOLDFISH are domesticated cousins of the carp. They can be found in many colours, shapes, and sizes.

Goosefish 3 ft. 4 in. *(1 m.)*
The GOOSEFISH is a kind of anglerfish with a wide, flat body. It can grow to be 4 ft. *(1·25 m.)* long.

Gopher, Pocket 8 in. *(20·3 cm.)*
The POCKET GOPHERS have furlined cheek pouches that open outside the mouth. In some places the name "gopher" is also used for ground squirrels, turtles, and other kinds of animals.

Gorilla over 6 ft. *(1·8 m.)* tall
The GORILLA is a peaceful animal, but its large size and powerful appearance have given it a false reputation as a fierce ape.

Grackle, Purple 1 ft. 5 in. *(43·1 cm.)*

The PURPLE GRACKLE'S feathers seem to change colour when seen at different angles.

Grasshopper 2 in. *(50·8 mm.)*

GRASSHOPPERS, with their long hind legs, can leap great distances. Many kinds also have wings and can fly when they want to travel a long way.

Grebe, Horned 1 ft. 1 in. *(33 cm.)*

The baby HORNED GREBE rides on its mother's back. Grebes are fine divers and swim rapidly underwater.

Green Turtle 4 ft. *(1·2 m.)*

The GREEN TURTLE'S worst enemy is man, who kills it for food and various other uses. It is now in danger of becoming extinct.

Green-bottle Fly ½ in. *(12·7 mm.)*
GREEN-BOTTLE FLIES look as if they were made of polished green metal. They buzz loudly when they fly.

Grizzly Bear 8 to 9 ft. *(2·4 to 2·7 m.)*
The GRIZZLY BEAR has a reputation for having a bad temper because it is solitary and resents intruders.

Grosbeak, Pine 9½ in. *(24·1 cm.)*
The PINE GROSBEAK has a powerful bill with which it can crack open hard-shelled seeds.

Grouper up to 6 ft. *(1·8 m.)*
GROUPERS are large sea fish that can weigh several hundred pounds. They are not dangerous and often show great curiosity about skin divers.

Grouse, Ruffed 1½ ft. *(45·7 cm.)*
The male RUFFED GROUSE makes a loud drumming sound with its wings to attract females.

Guinea Pig 1 ft. *(30·4 cm.)*
The GUINEA PIG is a domesticated version of a South American rodent called a cavy. Guinea pigs come in many colours and may have either long or short hair.

Gull, Herring 2 ft. *(60·9 cm.)*
The HERRING GULL opens clam-shells by dropping them from a great height on to a hard surface.

Gypsy Moth 2 in. *(50·8 mm.)* wingspan
The GYPSY MOTH was introduced to the United States many years ago. Today it is one of the country's most serious pests because its larvae feed on the leaves of fruit and shade trees.

Haddock 2 to $2\frac{1}{2}$ ft. *(60·9 to 76·2 cm.)*

The HADDOCK is an important food fish, like its cousin the cod. Small haddock are called scrod.

Halibut up to 8 ft. *(2·4 m.)* and over

The HALIBUT lives in very cold waters, sometimes at great depths.

Hammerhead Shark 8 to 15 ft. *(2·4 to 4·5 m.)*

The HAMMERHEAD SHARK'S eyes are located at the tips of its oddly shaped head. It is considered to be dangerous.

Hamster, European 11 in. *(27·9 cm.)*

The EUROPEAN HAMSTER is larger than the golden hamster so often kept as a pet. It too has cheek pouches used to carry seeds to its nest.

Harbour Seal 5 ft. *(1·5 m.)*

HARBOUR SEALS, unlike some of their shyer relatives, are sometimes seen around bays where there is great human activity. They like to rest on rocks off the shore.

Harpy Eagle 3 ft. 2 in. *(96·5 cm.)*

The HARPY EAGLE uses its powerful talons to capture monkeys, sloths, and other animals that it eats.

Hawk, Cooper's 1½ ft. *(45·7 cm.)*

The COOPER'S HAWK sometimes kills chickens, but it usually eats small rodents and wild birds.

Hedgehog, European 11 in. *(27·9 cm.)*

The EUROPEAN HEDGEHOG is covered with quills except on its belly. When attacked, it rolls into a spiny ball with its belly safely in the centre.

Hellbender 1 ft. 8 in. *(48·7 cm.)*

The HELLBENDER is a salamander that spends its entire life in rocky streams.

Hercules Beetle 6 in. *(15·2 cm.)*

The HERCULES BEETLE is one of the world's largest insects. The big horn is found only in the male.

Cooper's Hawk

European Hedgehog

Hellbender

Hercules Beetle

Nile Hippopotamus

Hermit Crab 3 in. *(76·2 mm.)* across

HERMIT CRABS have soft bodies and protect themselves by "wearing" empty seashells.

Heron, Great Blue 4 ft. 4 in. *(1·3 m.)*

The GREAT BLUE HERON is a very patient fisherman, waiting motionless in shallow water for a small fish or frog to come within range of its jabbing beak.

Herring 1 to $1\frac{1}{2}$ ft. *(30·4 to 45·7 cm.)*

HERRING are so numerous that they are an important part of the diet of many kinds of creatures, from gulls to seals.

Hippopotamus, Nile

up to 13 ft. *(3·9 m.)*

The NILE HIPPOPOTAMUS is found in most rivers of Africa. It passes the day in the water and comes up on land at night to feed.

Honey Badger $2\frac{1}{2}$ ft. *(76·2 cm.)*

Honey Guide $7\frac{1}{2}$ in. *(19 cm.)*

The HONEY BADGER is a large member of the weasel family. In some places it forms a partnership with the HONEY GUIDE, a bird that likes beeswax but is not strong enough to open a beehive. When a honey guide finds a hive, it makes a special call, and if a honey badger is near, it comes and tears open the hive. The badger eats the honey and the honey guide gets the wax.

Hornbill, Great 5 ft. *(1·5 m.)*

The female Great Hornbill, with some help from her mate, seals herself inside her nest chamber with a wall of mud until her eggs hatch. Her mate feeds her through a hole in the wall.

Hornet $\frac{3}{4}$ in. *(19 mm.)*

Hornets chew up wood to make a kind of paper with which they build their nests.

Horse, Mongolian Wild

6 ft. *(1·8 m.)*

The Mongolian Wild Horse is the only true wild horse living today except the zebra. It may already be extinct in the wild, but it is being preserved in zoos.

Mongolian Wild Horse (Przewalski)

Hornbill

Hornet

Horseshoe Crab

up to 2 ft. *(60·9 cm.)* long

HORSESHOE CRABS are not crabs at all, but marine cousins of the spiders.

House Spider $\frac{1}{4}$ in. *(6·3 mm.)*

HOUSE SPIDERS spin strong silk threads to make cobwebs, which are very different from the webs of garden spiders.

Howling Monkey 2 ft. 8 in. *(79·2 cm.)*

HOWLING MONKEYS have enlarged voice boxes that make their voices very loud. Groups of these monkeys calling can make the forest ring.

Hummingbird, Ruby-throated

$3\frac{1}{2}$ in. *(88·9 mm.)*

The RUBY-THROATED HUMMINGBIRD can fly backwards and up and down, like a helicopter. It is particularly attracted to red flowers and it sips their nectar.

Humpback Whale 40 ft. *(12·1 m.)*

The HUMPBACK WHALE is a medium-sized whale: it grows to a maximum length of about 50 ft. *(15 m.)*. Like other toothless whales, it eats huge quantities of tiny sea creatures, which it strains from the ocean through the flexible strips of whalebone in its upper jaw.

Hyena Spotted 3 ft. 4 in. *(1 m.)*

SPOTTED HYENAS have powerful teeth and jaws that can crack large bones. Sometimes they hunt for themselves and sometimes they eat what lions have left.

Ibex 4½ ft. *(1·3 m.)*

The IBEX is a wild goat that lives high in the mountains of Europe, Asia, and North Africa. The male has enormous, gently curving horns.

Ibis, Scarlet 2 ft. *(60·9 cm.)*

The SCARLET IBIS probes in the mud for insects and other small water creatures to eat.

Ichneumon Fly 1½ in. *(38·1 mm.)*

ICHNEUMON FLIES drill through bark with their long egg-laying organs and deposit their eggs in the bodies of wood-boring insects.

Iguana, Common 6 ft. *(1·8 m.)*

The COMMON IGUANA is bright emerald green when it is young, but becomes greyish green as it grows up. Full-grown iguanas can be 6 ft. *(1·8 m.)* long.

Impala 4 ft. *(1·2 m.)*

Only male IMPALAS have horns. These graceful antelope can make great leaps when they are frightened.

Imperial Moth

4 6/10 in. *(116 mm.)* wingspan

The IMPERIAL MOTH, which is very large, is closely related to the silk moth. In its caterpillar stage it is covered with hair and feeds on almost any kind of tree leaf.

Inchworm 1 in. *(25·4 mm.)*

INCHWORMS are the caterpillars of small moths. When frightened, inchworms stop moving and masquerade as twigs.

Jackal 2 ft. 2 in. *(66 cm.)*

Like most members of the dog family, JACKALS hunt a variety of small animals. They also hang around lions' kills and sneak a bite when they can.

Alpine Ibex
Scarlet Ibis
Ichneumon Fly
Inchworm
Common Iguana
Side-striped Jackal
Impala
Imperial Moth

Jack Rabbit 2 ft. *(60·9 cm.)*

JACK RABBITS are not really rabbits but hares. Their young are born able to see and to run.

Jaguar 6 to 8 ft. *(1·8 to 2·4 m.)*

The JAGUAR is the largest of the American cats. It looks something like a heavy leopard, but its spots usually have smaller spots inside.

Jaguarondi 2 to 2½ ft. *(60·9 to 76·2 cm.)*

JAGUARONDIS come in two colours, red and grey. At one time it was thought that these were separate species, but both colours can be found in a single litter.

Japanese Beetle ½ in. *(12·7 mm.)*

The JAPANESE BEETLE was introduced to the United States accidentally and quickly became a pest. Now it is controlled to some extent by an imported Japanese wasp that feeds on it.

Jay, Blue 1 ft. *(30·4 cm.)*

The lively BLUE JAY likes to taunt cats and other animals that hunt birds. It eats many things, from insects to acorns.

Jellyfish up to 1 ft. *(30·4 cm.)* across, tentacles up to 12 ft. *(3·6 m.)*

JELLYFISHES propel themselves through the water by contracting and relaxing their bell-shaped bodies.

Jerboa 5 in. *(12·7 cm.)*

JERBOAS hop like tiny kangaroos and live in the desert. They spend the day in their burrows to escape the heat.

June Beetle 1 in. *(25·4 mm.)*

JUNE BEETLES stay underground during the day and come out at night to feed on leaves.

Kangaroo, Red 6 ft. *(1·8 m.)*

Only adult male RED KANGAROOS are red; females are bluish grey.

Katydid $1\frac{3}{10}$ in. *(33 mm.)*

Male KATYDIDS have ridges on their front wings; when rubbed together, these ridges make the familiar sound heard in late summer in North America.

Kea 1 ft. 7 in. *(48·2 cm.)*

The KEA, like most parrots, was originally a fruit eater, but it has learned to eat meat in the wild and has been accused of killing sheep.

Killdeer 10 in. *(25·4 cm.)*

When someone approaches a KILLDEER'S nest, the female rushes away acting as if her wing were broken, thus taking attention away from her eggs.

Killer Whale 30 ft. *(9·1 m.)*

KILLER WHALES live in packs and sometimes attack and kill larger whales. They are very intelligent and can be easily trained in captivity.

Kingfisher, Belted 1 ft. 1 in. *(33 cm.)*

BELTED KINGFISHERS make their homes in burrows in the banks of rivers. They spend much time sitting on branches above the water, waiting to swoop down and catch a fish.

Kinkajou 1 ft. 9 in. *(53·3 cm.)*

The KINKAJOU is an odd cousin of the raccoon. Like some monkeys, it can hang by its strong tail.

Kite, Everglade $1\frac{1}{2}$ ft. *(45·7 cm.)*

The EVERGLADE KITE eats nothing but a certain kind of snail, which it pulls out of the shell with its hooked beak.

Kiwi 2 ft. 4 in. *(70·1 cm.)*

The KIWI has tiny wings that are useless for flying. It is most active at night.

Koala $2\frac{1}{2}$ ft. *(76·2 cm.)*

A young KOALA too large to fit in its mother's pouch rides on her back.

Kudu, Greater 8 ft. *(2·4 m.)*, 4 ft. 3 in. *(1·2 m.)* at shoulders

The GREATER KUDU has large corkscrew horns and white stripes on its body.

Lacewing, Green 1 in. *(25·4 mm.)*

The GREEN LACEWING gives off a foul-smelling liquid to protect itself when it is handled.

Ladybird $\frac{3}{10}$ in. *(7·6 mm.)*

LADYBIRDS are beneficial to farmers because they eat other insects that feed on crops.

Lamprey up to 3 ft. *(91·4 cm.)*

LAMPREYS are fishes that have no jaws. They have circular mouths with horny teeth, with which they hang on to other fishes and suck their blood.

Lapwing 1 ft. *(30·4 cm.)*

The LAPWING is a cousin of the killdeer. It often flies with a peculiar twisting and turning motion.

Lark, Horned 7 in. *(17·7 cm.)*

The HORNED LARK is not a lark, but a member of the blackbird family. Its horns are really feathers.

Leatherback Turtle 8 ft. *(2·4 m.)*

The LEATHERBACK TURTLE is the largest of all turtles and can weigh as much as 100 lb. *(450 kgm.)*. It lives in the sea.

Lemming 5 in. *(12·7 cm.)*

LEMMINGS are small rodents well known for their population explosions. At such times millions seek new living space, and many drown while trying to swim the sea.

Lemur 2 ft. 3 in. *(68·5 cm.)*

Most LEMURS, cousins of the monkeys, are awake only at night, but the RING-TAILED LEMUR is active in the daytime.

Leopard 4 to 5 ft. *(1·2 to 1·5 m.)*

The LEOPARD can live in forests and open plains. It often drags its kill up into a tree for safekeeping.

Leopard Seal 10 ft. *(3 m.)*

The LEOPARD SEAL is the only seal known that regularly eats penguins.

Lesser Panda 2 ft. *(60·9 cm.)*

The LESSER PANDA, which lives in Asia, is a member of the raccoon family. It eats leaves and fruit and is an agile tree climber.

Limpet 5 in. *(12·7 cm.)*

LIMPETS are related to snails. They spend most of their time on rocks in the water.

Limpkin 2 ft. 1 in. *(63·5 cm.)*

Snails are the LIMPKIN'S favourite food. The limpkin is one of the few birds active at night, and its loud cries fill the air of southern swamps in America.

Lion 6½ ft. *(1·9 m.)*

Unlike other cats, LIONS live in groups that are called prides. Only the males have manes, and a large male may weigh 500 lb. *(225 kgm.)*.

Lizard, Collared 1 ft. 3 in. *(38·1 cm.)*
The COLLARED LIZARD usually walks on all four feet, like most other lizards; but when it is in a hurry it runs on its hind legs.

Llama 4 ft. *(1·2 m.)* at the shoulders
Like its Old World relations the camels, the LLAMA has been domesticated and is used for food, wool, and transportation.

Lobster 1 ft. *(30·4 cm.)*
The LOBSTER usually walks at a slow pace on the sea floor, but to escape its enemies it swims rapidly—backwards!

Locust 3 in. *(76·2 mm.)*
LOCUSTS are grasshoppers. Now and then their numbers increase, and swarms, or "plagues", of locusts move into new territory, often damaging crops.

Loon 3 ft. *(91·4 cm.)*
The LOON is an expert diver. It can hold its breath underwater for many minutes at a time.

Loris, Slow 1 ft. 3 in. *(38·1 cm.)*
The SLOW LORIS' name means "clown" and refers to the odd markings on its face.

Lory 11 in. *(27·9 cm.)*
The LORY has a tongue with a brushlike edge, which it uses to lap up the juice of flowers it crushes in its beak.

Louse $\frac{1}{8}$ in. *(3 mm.)*

A LOUSE is a very small wingless insect that lives on warm-blooded animals. Some lice carry disease, while others are just annoying.

Lovebird 5 in. *(12·7 cm.)*

Some kinds of LOVEBIRDS carry bits of nesting material in their rump feathers instead of in their beaks.

Lumpfish up to 1 ft. 8 in. *(50·8 cm.)*

LUMPFISH cling to rocks by means of suction disks on their undersides.

Luna Moth $3\frac{1}{4}$ in. *(82·5 mm.)* wingspan

The beautiful LUNA MOTH is named after the moon (*luna*) because of the yellow circles on its wings. The larvae feed on leaves and on persimmons.

Lungfish 6 ft. *(1·8 m.)*

Like land animals, LUNGFISH breathe air and can drown if kept underwater too long.

Lynx 3 ft. *(91·4 cm.)*

The LYNX has enormous feet that in winter act like snowshoes.

Lyrebird 3 ft. 2 in. *(96·5 cm.)*

The LYREBIRD builds its nest on the ground, with a roof and walls. It is named after the lyre because its tail feathers resemble the musical instrument.

Macaw, Military 2½ ft. *(76·2 cm.)*

The MILITARY MACAW is one of the largest and most colourful parrots.

Mackerel, Atlantic 1 ft. *(30·4 cm.)*

The ATLANTIC MACKEREL feeds mostly on tiny sea creatures called plankton.

Magpie 1½ ft. *(45·7 cm.)*

MAGPIES, like their close relatives crows and jays, are very clever birds. They sometimes sit on the backs of deer and pick off insect pests.

Malayan Sun Bear 4½ ft. *(1·3 m.)*

The MALAYAN SUN BEAR is the smallest of the bears. Its short, sleek coat is very different from the shaggy fur of other kinds of bears.

Mallard 2 ft. 4 in. *(70·1 cm.)*

The MALLARD is one of the most familiar ducks in the world. It is the ancestor of many domestic breeds.

Mamba, Green 10 ft. *(3 m.)*

The GREEN MAMBA is one of the deadliest of snakes. Fortunately for man, it spends much of its time in trees, hunting for birds and lizards.

Manatee 12 ft. *(3·6 m.)*

The MANATEE, an aquatic mammal related to the dugong, can stay underwater as long as fifteen minutes without breathing. This sociable creature lives in warm seas.

Mandrill over 3 ft. *(91·4 cm.)*

Young MANDRILL males look like females. Not until they grow up do they develop the typical bold colours on face and rump.

Manta Ray over 20 ft. *(6 m.)* across

The MANTA RAY is the largest of all the rays. Like its cousins the sharks, it has a rubbery skeleton made of cartilage rather than bone.

Mantis, Praying 3½ in. *(88·9 mm.)*

The PRAYING MANTIS uses only its lower two pairs of legs for walking, and snatches insects with the upper pair. The way it holds this pair of legs while waiting for a victim makes it look as if it were praying.

Marmoset 1 ft. 2 in. *(35·5 cm.)*

MARMOSETS have retractable claws instead of fingernails. The male usually carries the babies on his back and gives them to the mother only for feeding.

Marmot 2 ft. 5 in. *(73·6 cm.)*

MARMOTS are big ground-living squirrels. Marmots (including the woodchucks) hibernate in winter.

Marten 2 ft. *(60·9 cm.)*

MARTENS, as much at home high in a tree as on the ground, move swiftly enough to prey on squirrels.

Meerkat 1 ft. 1 in. *(33 cm.)*

The MEERKAT is a mongoose, but unlike its unsociable relatives, it lives in groups. Meerkats eat many things and are particularly fond of insects.

Merganser, Hooded 1½ ft. *(45·7 cm.)*

The HOODED MERGANSER is more often seen than its relatives because it is not so shy. It eats small fish and crayfish.

Millipede up to 7 in. *(17·7 cm.)*

Some kinds of MILLIPEDES ooze an irritating chemical when they are attacked by ants. The chemical gas hangs in the air while the millipede crawls away to safety.

Mink up to 2 ft. *(60·9 cm.)*

The MINK lives near water, where it can catch frogs and other small creatures. Its fur is so valuable that millions of mink are now raised on ranches to make coats.

Minnow 2 to 4 in. *(50·8 to 101·6 mm.)*

Most kinds of MINNOWS have no teeth in their mouths, but instead have toothlike structures near their gills.

Mite $\frac{1}{20}$ in. *(1·2 mm.)*

All but a few kinds of MITES are so small that they cannot be seen with the naked eye.

Mockingbird $10\frac{1}{2}$ in. *(26·6 cm.)*

MOCKINGBIRDS are expert impersonators; not only do they sing their own songs, but they can imitate the songs of many other kinds of birds.

Mole, Star-nosed $4\frac{1}{2}$ in. *(114·3 mm.)*

The fleshy nose "star" of the STAR-NOSED MOLE is made up of feelers. Like other kinds of moles, it has shovel-shaped front feet and digs through the soil in search of insects and worms.

Monarch Butterfly

4 in. *(101 mm.)* wingspan

MONARCH BUTTERFLIES migrate south for the winter and return to the north in the spring, like some birds.

Mongoose, Indian 2 ft. *(60·9 cm.)*

The INDIAN MONGOOSE, though famous as a killer of cobras, usually hunts rodents and birds.

Monitor, Komodo 10 ft. *(3 m.)*

The KOMODO MONITOR, which may be 10 ft. *(3 m.)* long, is the largest lizard in the world. It has a forked tongue like a snake.

Monkey, Moustache 2 ft. *(60·9 cm.)*

MOUSTACHE MONKEYS have bright-blue faces. Bright colours are usual among guenons, the group to which these monkeys belong.

Moose

9 ft. *(2·7 m.)*, 7 ft. *(2·1 m.)* at the shoulders

The MOOSE is the largest of all deer. It is fond of water and likes to go into ponds in summer to escape biting flies.

Moray Eel 6 ft. *(1·8 m.)*

MORAY EELS are fierce fish that lie in underwater crevices, waiting to dart after prey.

Mosquito $\frac{3}{10}$ in. *(7·6 mm.)*

Only the female MOSQUITO bites humans and animals; the male feeds on plant juices.

Mourning Cloak Butterfly

$2\frac{6}{10}$ in. wingspan *(66 mm.)*

The MOURNING CLOAK BUTTERFLY hibernates in winter, but during a mild spell it sometimes awakens and flies about.

Mouse, House $3\frac{1}{2}$ in. *(88·9 mm.)*

The HOUSE MOUSE, usually considered a pest, has followed man all over the world. On the other hand, specially bred varieties used in laboratories have been very useful in medical research.

Mouse, Pocket 6 in. *(15·2 cm.)*

The POCKET MOUSE, a distant relative of the house mouse, lives in the desert, where there is very little water. It makes drinking water from the fatty substances in the seeds it eats.

Mosquito

Alaskan Moose

Moustache Monkey

Mourning Cloak Butterfly

House Mouse

Pocket Mouse

Moray Eel

Myna Bird

Mouse Deer (Chevrotain)

Mud Puppy

Common Murre

Muskrat

Musk Ox

Mouse Deer 1 ft. 8 in. *(50·8 cm.)*

MOUSE DEER are not really deer, but are related to camels and pigs. The males have long tusks.

Mud Puppy 1 ft. *(30·4 cm.)*

The MUD PUPPY is a salamander that spends its entire life in the water. Most kinds of salamanders lose their gills and become air breathers on land when they grow up.

Murre 1 ft. 5 in. *(43·1 cm.)*

The COMMON MURRE gets its name from its call, *murrrr*. This diving bird is known by many other names too: "scuttock", "tinker", and "frowl".

Musk Ox 6½ ft. *(1·9 m.)*

When herds of MUSK OXEN are threatened, they form a circle with their heads facing out. The calves are protected inside the circle, and the musk oxen's sharp horns keep attackers from getting through.

Muskrat 1 ft. *(30·4 cm.)*

The MUSKRAT, whose webbed feet make it a good swimmer, lives in a den built of water plants.

Myna Bird 1 ft. 1 in. *(33 cm.)*

Like parrots, MYNA BIRDS make interesting pets because they can learn to imitate human speech.

Narwhal 15 ft. *(4·5 m.)*, tooth 9 ft. *(2·7 m.)*

The NARWHAL'S "horn" is an enormous tooth that grows forward from its snout. Early explorers, seeing the tusk, believed it was a unicorn's horn.

Native Cat 1 ft. 4 in. *(39·6 m.)*

The first Englishmen to visit Australia called the dasyure a NATIVE CAT because they did not realize that almost all the mammals there were related to the opossums.

Nautilus, Chambered 5 in. *(12·7 cm.)*

As it grows, the CHAMBERED NAUTILUS adds larger sections to its shell and lives in the outermost and largest section.

Nene 2 ft. 4 in. *(70·1 cm.)*

Man and his animals almost made the NENE extinct in its native Hawaii. It is now protected, and a few pairs, sent to Slimbridge, England, have multiplied very well.

Newt, Eastern 3 in. *(76·2 mm.)*

Although the EASTERN NEWT breathes air, it spends its adult life in ponds, after living for a while on land as a red eft.

Night Heron 2 ft. 4 in. *(70·1 cm.)*

The NIGHT HERON roosts in trees all day and feeds when it gets dark. It makes a hoarse *quock, quock* as it flies.

Nightingale $6\frac{1}{2}$ in. *(16·5 cm.)*

The NIGHTINGALE is not a very pretty bird, but its song is one of the most beautiful in the world.

Nuthatch 6 in. *(15·2 cm.)*

The NUTHATCH likes to creep up and down tree trunks looking for spiders, insects, or seeds. It often hangs head down.

Nyala

5 ft. *(1·5 m.)*, horns over 2 ft. *(60·9 cm.)*

The female NYALA antelope has a smooth tan coat and no horns, while the male has large horns and a shaggy grey coat.

Oarfish

up to 30 ft. *(9·1 m.)*

The strange OARFISH is more than 20 ft. *(6 m.)* long and has no tail fin. Occasional glimpses of it may have led people to believe that they had seen a sea serpent.

Ocelot

3 ft. 4 in. *(1 m.)*

The OCELOT is one of the smallest of the American spotted cats. Its fur is so much in demand that thousands are killed each year.

Octopus

5 in. *(12·7 cm.)* to 28 ft. *(8·5 m.)*

The OCTOPUS has eight tentacles and can move very fast. When threatened, it squirts out an inky fluid to confuse the enemy.

Okapi

7 ft. *(2·1 m)*, 5 ft. *(1·5 m.)* at the shoulders

The OKAPI is closely related to the giraffe, but it has a short neck and can move easily among the low branches in a forest. It eats leaves and twigs, wrapping its long tongue around branches and pulling them to its mouth.

Onager 6½ ft. *(1·9 m.)*

The ONAGER, a wild ass, lives in dry, desert areas where there are few people, and this is probably why it has continued to exist, for its wild Eurasian cousins have all been killed by hunters.

Opaleye 1 ft. 8 in. *(48·7 cm.)*

The OPALEYE lives along the rocky shores of the southern California coast. Its bluish-green eyes gave it its name.

Opossum 1 ft. 8 in. *(48·7 cm.)*

An OPOSSUM'S babies, sometimes as many as eighteen, are smaller than a honeybee. The mother generally carries them in her abdominal pouch.

Orang-utan up to 5 ft. *(1·5 m.)*

The ORANG-UTAN, an ape almost as big as a gorilla, is becoming extinct as men cut down the forests that are its home.

Oriole, Baltimore 7½ in. *(19 cm.)*

The BALTIMORE ORIOLE'S nest is shaped like a sack and hangs from a branch high in a tree.

Oryx 6 ft. *(1·8 m.)* at the shoulders

ORYXES are large antelope with long, slightly curved horns that are used as defensive weapons.

Opaleye

Baltimore Oriole

Beisa Oryx

Opossum

Onager

Orang-utan

Osprey 2 ft. *(60·9 cm.)*

An OSPREY hovering high above the water can spot a fish, dive, and catch it in its sharp claws. Bald eagles sometimes chase ospreys until they drop their fish, which the eagles catch in the air.

Ostrich 6 ft. *(1·8 m.)*

The OSTRICH is the largest bird in the world. Contrary to legend, it does not bury its head in the sand to escape its enemies: it crouches low or runs swiftly away.

Otter 3 ft. 4 in. *(1 m.)*

Because OTTERS are so expert at catching crayfish and slower fishes, they have lots of time for their favourite activity—playing.

Ounce 3 ft. 9 in. *(1·1 m.)*

The OUNCE, or snow leopard, lives in high Asian mountains. Its long coat protects it from the cold.

Owl, Barn 1 ft. 3 in. *(38·1 cm.)*

The BARN OWL'S ears are hidden under the feathers of its face disc. Its hearing is so acute that even in total darkness it can locate a mouse that makes the slightest noise and pounce on it.

Oyster 6 in. *(15·2 cm.)*

Not all kinds of OYSTERS produce valuable pearls. Pearls made by the kind of oyster we eat are worth very little.

Paca $2\frac{1}{2}$ ft. *(76·2 cm.)*

The PACA is not a sociable creature. Each one lives in its own burrow and comes out to feed at night.

Painted Lady

$2\frac{2}{10}$ in. *(55·8 mm.)* wingspan

PAINTED LADIES are active all summer long and then sleep through the winter.

Painted Turtle

5 to 6 in. *(12·7 to 15·2 cm.)*

PAINTED TURTLES, with their bright-red markings at the edge of the shell, are the commonest turtles in eastern North America. They rest in the sun on rocks and logs and plunge into the water if disturbed.

Panda, Giant 5 ft. 6 in. *(1·6 m.)*

The GIANT PANDA, despite its stumpy tail and 300 lb. *(135 kgm.)* bulk, is not a bear but a raccoon. It lives in a small area of the mountains of western China, where its favourite food—the bamboo tree—grows.

Pangolin 3 ft. *(91·4 cm.)*

PANGOLINS are like the true ant-eaters in habits and shape, except for their coat of large scales, which makes them look like walking pine cones.

Parakeet, Shell 7 in. *(17·7 cm.)*

Wild SHELL PARAKEETS, or budgerigars, are green, but pet fanciers have developed dozens of other colours through captive breeding.

Parrot, African Grey

1 ft. 1 in. *(33 cm.)*

Of all the many kinds of parrots, the AFRICAN GREY PARROT is considered to be the best talker.

Partridge, Hungarian

1 ft. 1 in. *(33 cm.)*

The HUNGARIAN PARTRIDGE was introduced into North America as a game bird. In most places it did not survive, but in the Great Plains it was able to live where other game birds could not and is now thriving.

Peacock 7½ ft. *(2·2 m.)*

The PEACOCK'S tail is actually quite small and is hidden by the huge and colourful rump feathers that most persons call the tail. The female is called a peahen.

Peccary, Collared 3 ft. *(91·4 cm.)*

The COLLARED PECCARY has a small scent gland on its back. When it is excited, the peccary gives off a strong odour. A group of these pig-like animals can put an enemy to flight.

Pelican, Brown 4 ft. 2 in. *(1·2 m.)*

BROWN PELICANS dive from the air to catch fishes in their enormous beaks.

Penguin 4 ft. *(1·2 m.)*

Most PENGUINS live in the Antarctic. They eat fishes, which they catch by "flying" underwater—at speeds up to 30 m.p.h. *(48 km.p.h.)*—with their stubby, flipperlike wings, which are useless in the air. Largest of the penguins, the EMPEROR stands over 3 ft. *(91·4 cm.)* tall. The ADÉLIE PENGUIN is about 2 ft. *(60 cm.)* tall. Both kinds travel miles from the sea to their nesting grounds.

Perch, Yellow 1 ft. *(30·4 cm)*

The YELLOW PERCH is one of the commonest fishes in North American lakes.

Periwinkle $2\frac{1}{2}$ in. *(63·5 mm.)*

PERIWINKLES are sea snails that live in tidal pools and eat plants.

Pheasant 3 ft. *(91·4 cm.)*

Male PHEASANTS have long, graceful tails and bright colours. The RING-NECKED PHEASANT has been taken to many parts of the world from its native Asia.

Pigeon, Crowned 2 ft. 9 in. *(83·8 cm.)*

The CROWNED PIGEON is a giant among pigeons: it is nearly 3 ft. *(91·4 cm.)* long.

Pika 8 in. *(20·3 cm.)*

PIKAS, short-eared cousins of the rabbits, live in mountain rockslides. They store green plants, let them dry out, and use them for winter food.

Pipit $6\frac{1}{2}$ in. *(16·5 cm.)*

PIPITS never hop, but run about catching insects on the ground. They get their name from their soft, unchanging song—*pip-it, pip-it.*

Piranha $10\frac{1}{2}$ in. *(26·6 cm.)*

A school of small PIRANHAS, with their sharp teeth, will attack even large animals and strip them to the bone.

Platypus 1 ft. 8 in. *(48·7 cm.)*

The unusual PLATYPUS pokes its rubbery, duck-like beak through river mud in search of crayfish and worms at night and sleeps during the day. The female lays eggs and nurses her babies.

Plover, Golden 10 in. *(25·4 cm.)*

Each year the GOLDEN PLOVER flies nearly 3,000 miles *(4825 km.)* from its breeding grounds in Labrador to Argentina and back again—non-stop each way.

Polar Bear 8½ to 11 ft. *(2·5 to 3·3 m.)*

The mother POLAR BEAR gives birth to her cubs in a den dug in a snowdrift. Although the full-grown polar bear weighs over half a ton, a baby at birth weighs only a pound or two.

Polecat, European 1½ ft. *(45·7 cm.)*

The EUROPEAN POLECAT is the wild ancestor of the domesticated ferret.

Polyphemus Moth

5¼ in. *(13·3 cm.)* wingspan

The caterpillar of the POLYPHEMUS MOTH spins a large silken cocoon.

Pompano 1 ft. *(30·4 cm.)*

POMPANO often frequent the mouths of rivers and are among the more difficult fishes to catch.

Porcupine, North American

2½ ft. *(76·2 cm.)*

The NORTH AMERICAN PORCUPINE is very fond of salt. It sometimes gnaws axe handles that have soaked up salty perspiration.

Porgy $2\frac{1}{2}$ ft. *(76·2 cm.)*

PORGIES have two kinds of teeth: sharp front teeth for biting and broad back teeth for grinding shellfish. The SHEEPSHEAD is one of the largest of porgies.

Porpoise, Common 4 to 6 ft. *(1·2 to 1·8 m.)*

COMMON PORPOISES are only about 6 ft. *(1·8 m.)* long. They live in groups, often near the mouths of rivers, and sometimes swim some distance upriver.

Potto 1 ft. *(30·4 cm.)*

The POTTO, a slow-moving cousin of the bush babies, is a night prowler whose bite is very difficult to shake loose.

Prairie Dog 1 ft. 2 in. *(35·5 cm.)*

PRAIRIE DOGS live in large colonies, which once covered great areas, and their tunnels are sometimes shared by owls, gopher tortoises, and rattlesnakes. Prairie dogs, actually ground squirrels, were named for their call, which sounds like a dog barking.

Prawn $1\frac{1}{2}$ in. *(38·1 mm.)*

PRAWNS are close relatives of shrimp and lobsters, and like them, they are often eaten by man.

Proboscis Monkey 2 ft. 4 in. *(70·1 cm.)*

The PROBOSCIS MONKEY can swim—an unusual ability for a monkey—and lives along rivers. Only the adult male has the big nose.

Pronghorn 4 ft. *(1·2 m.)*

The PRONGHORN is found only in North America. It is the one horned animal that sheds its horn each year the way a deer sheds its antlers. It sheds only the horny outer covering, however, not the bony core.

Ptarmigan 1 ft. 3 in. *(38·1 cm.)*

The PTARMIGAN wears white feathers in winter and brown ones in summer. It lives on berries and other parts of plants.

Puffbird 7 in. *(17·7 cm.)*

PUFFBIRDS like to sit quietly, waiting for insects to come along. When one does, a puffbird will dart out and catch it.

Puffin 1 ft. *(30·4 cm.)*

PUFFINS' bills grow a brightly coloured outer layer—which is later lost—in the breeding season. Puffins lay their eggs in burrows.

Puma 7 ft. *(2·1 m.)*

The PUMA was once found throughout the Western Hemisphere, but it has been wiped out in most of North America. The puma is known by many other names, such as "cougar", "painter", "catamount", and "mountain lion".

Pygmy Hippopotamus 5 ft. *(1·5 m.)*

The PYGMY HIPPOPOTAMUS spends less time in the water than the big hippo and is more solitary in its habits. A full-grown pygmy weighs only about 500 lb. *(225 kgm.)*.

Python 19 to 28 ft. *(5·7 to 8·5 m.)*

PYTHONS are among the largest snakes in the world. Some of them become very tame in zoos.

Quahog 3 in. *(76·2 mm.)*

QUAHOGS are a favourite food today, as they were in Indian times. Great piles of shells can still be found on the coasts, where the refuse heaps of Indian villages were once located.

Quail, California 11 in. *(27·9 cm.)*

The CALIFORNIA QUAIL has managed to adjust to man and can be seen in suburban back gardens and even in some city parks.

Quetzal 3 ft. 2 in. *(96·5 cm.)*

The beautiful QUETZAL was worshiped as the god of the air by the ancient Mayas and Aztecs.

Rabbit, European Wild

1 ft. 8 in. *(50·8 cm.)*

The EUROPEAN WILD RABBIT is the ancestor of our domestic breeds of rabbits, some of which are much larger than the wild one.

Raccoon 2 ft. 8 in. *(81·2 cm.)*

The RACCOON often drops its food in water and plays with it, a performance that looks as if the raccoon were washing its food.

Rail, Virginia 10 in. *(25·4 cm.)*

The thin body of the VIRGINIA RAIL enables it to slip between the stems of marsh reeds.

Rat, Black 8 in. *(20·3 cm.)*

The BLACK RAT, or roof rat, is more common in warm climates than its larger cousin the Norway rat. It is a serious pest.

Rattlesnake, Diamondback

5 ft. *(1·5 m.)*

The DIAMONDBACK RATTLESNAKE can grow to be 8 ft. *(2·5 m.)* long and weighs more than any venomous snake in the world. It usually, but not always, warns an intruder before biting by vigorously shaking the horny rattle on its tail.

Rat Kangaroo $1\frac{1}{2}$ ft. *(45·7 cm.)*

RAT KANGAROOS are very small kangaroos. They are often active at night.

Raven 2 ft. *(60·9 cm.)*

In spite of its intelligence, the RAVEN has not been able to get along near man, as the crow has, and it now lives only in remote places.

Ray (Stingray) 2 to 7 ft. *(60·9 cm. to 2·1 m.)* across

The STINGRAY has a poisonous spine in its tail. If disturbed, it can whip its tail around and drive the spine into an enemy.

Redstart 5 in. *(12·7 cm.)*

The REDSTART uses grass, bark, and spider webs to make its nest.

Reindeer 6 ft. *(1·8 m.)*

Both male and female REINDEER have antlers, like their wild ancestors the caribou. The female's antlers are smaller than her mate's but larger than those of the males in some other species.

Remora 2 ft. *(60·9 cm.)*

The REMORA has a big suction disc by which it attaches itself to sharks and sea turtles. Not only does it get a free ride, but it eats scraps of food that are missed by its carrier.

Rhea 4 ft. 4 in. *(1·3 m.)*

Male RHEAS mate with half a dozen females, which then lay their eggs in one nest. The male incubates the eggs—twenty or more—by himself and then takes care of them.

Rhesus Monkey 2 ft. *(60·9 cm.)*

The RHESUS MONKEY has blood groups very similar to man's and has been important in medical research.

Rhinoceros Beetle $2\frac{1}{2}$ in. *(63·5 mm.)*

Only the male RHINOCEROS BEETLE has two large, hornlike spines. The female has just a hint of one horn on her head.

Rhinoceros, Black up to 11 ft. *(3·3 m.)*

The BLACK RHINOCEROS has two horns that continue to grow all its life. The rhino keeps them trimmed by rubbing them on trees and rocks.

Roadrunner 2 ft. *(60·9 cm.)*

The ROADRUNNER, a cousin of the cuckoo, eats insects, scorpions, and small snakes.

Robin, American 10 in. *(25·4 cm.)*

The AMERICAN ROBIN is really a thrush, but it looks so much like the robin of England that early settlers gave it the same name.

Rocky Mountain Goat 5 ft. *(1·5 m.)*

The ROCKY MOUNTAIN GOAT is a goat-antelope so sure-footed that it can live in very steep places. The kid can climb with its mother when it is only a few days old.

Rose Chafer ½ in. *(12·7 mm.)*

ROSE CHAFERS feed on a variety of flowers in addition to roses.

Royal Antelope 1 ft. 7 in. *(48·2 cm.)*

The ROYAL ANTELOPE, 10 in. *(25·4 cm.)* tall at the shoulder, is the world's smallest antelope, but it can make 9 ft. *(2·75 m.)* jumps.

Ruff 1 ft. *(30·4 cm.)*

The male RUFF'S fringe of long neck feathers grows only during the mating season. The female is called a reeve.

Saiga Antelope
4 to 5 ft. *(1·2 to 1·5 m.)*

The SAIGA ANTELOPE'S swollen nose, which overhangs its nostrils and shelters them, may help it survive on the cold plains of Russia.

Sailfish
up to 11 ft. *(3·3 m.)*

When it wants to swim rapidly, the SAILFISH folds its high, sail-like dorsal fin down into a slot on its back.

Saki
2 ft. 2 in. *(66 cm.)*

SAKIS are rarely seen in zoos because they are so delicate that few survive captivity. Sakis sometimes catch and eat sleeping bats, but their chief food is fruit.

Salamander
7 in. *(17·7 cm.)*

Most SALAMANDERS prefer darkness to light. The CAVE SALAMANDER lives in the "twilight zone", where there is some faint daylight. The SPOTTED SALAMANDER hides under rocks by day and comes out to hunt insects at night.

Salmon, Chinook
2 ft. *(60·9 cm.)*

The CHINOOK SALMON is the largest kind of salmon. Its meat is eaten and its eggs are used for caviar.

Sand Dollar
2 to $2\frac{1}{2}$ in. *(50·8 to 63·5 mm.)*

SAND DOLLARS are cousins of the starfish. Their sun-bleached shells are often seen at the seashore.

Sandpiper, Spotted
8 in. *(20·3 cm.)*

The SPOTTED SANDPIPER loses its spots in the fall, but it can still be identified by the way it pumps its tail up and down.

Sargassum Fish
6 in. *(15·2 cm.)*

The SARGASSUM FISH is camouflaged to resemble the stringy seaweed in which it waits motionless for small fishes to come near.

Sawfish 16 to 20 ft. *(4·8 to 6 m.)*
The Sawfish uses its snout to stun other fishes.

Scallop 1 to 4 in. *(25·4 to 101·6 mm.)*
Scallops have many small blue eyes just inside the outer edge of their shells.

Scarab Beetle 1 in. *(25·4 mm.)*
Scarab Beetles have played a great role in the religion and art of ancient Egypt. One kind forms a ball of cow droppings, rolls it about, and then lays its eggs inside.

Scorpion 3 to 8 in. *(76·2 mm. to 20·3 cm.)*
The tail sting of the Scorpion is painful but usually not fatal to humans. In spite of this weapon, many scorpions are eaten by small animals and birds.

Screamer 2 ft. 4 in. *(70·1 cm.)*
Screamers, with their loud screams, often warn other animals that hunters are approaching. They have sharp, horny spurs at the front of their wings.

Screech Owl 10 in. *(25·4 cm.)*
Screech Owls can be found in two colours, grey and red. Because the owls are colour-blind, they look alike to one another.

Sea Horse
2 to 8 in. *(50·4 mm. to 20·3 cm.)*
The male Sea Horse incubates his mate's eggs in a pouch on his belly, and the young stay there for a while after they hatch.

Sea Otter 4½ ft. *(1·3 m.)*
The Sea Otter places a stone from the ocean floor on its chest and breaks open mussel shells by hammering them on the stone.

Sea Lion, California 8 ft. *(2·4 m.)*

The CALIFORNIA SEA LION swims with powerful strokes of its front flippers. Its cheerful bark is familiar in zoos all over the world.

Secretary Bird 3 ft. 10 in. *(1·1 m.)*

The SECRETARY BIRD stalks through tall grass searching for snakes to eat.

Serval 2½ ft. *(76·2 cm.)*

The SERVAL is an expert leaper and can catch birds as they fly up in front of it.

Sewellel 1 ft. 3 in. *(38·1 cm.)*

The SEWELLEL, or mountain beaver, a stubby-tailed distant relative of the true beaver, lives in burrows in the cool forests of the Pacific Northwest. Mice and shrews often use the sewellel's tunnels.

Shark 12 to 36 ft. *(3·6 to 10·9 m.)*

SHARKS range in size from small dogfish to the 50 ft. *(15 m.)* long but harmless whale shark. Some, like the GREAT WHITE SHARK, have no fear of man and will attack swimmers.

Shoebill 4 ft. *(1·2 m.)*

The SHOEBILL, or whale-headed, stork eats a variety of creatures, including small crocodiles.

Shrew 5 in. *(12·7 cm.)*

SHREWS, tiny and hyper-active, must eat very often, for they burn up energy at a rapid rate. One kind, the MUSK SHREW, sometimes lives in houses; it eats insects and gives off a strong smell.

Shrike 9½ in. *(24·1 cm.)*

SHRIKES eat other small birds. They often impale their victims on a thorn or on barbed wire.

Shrimp 1 to 3 in. *(25·4 to 76·2 mm.)*

Some SHRIMP make snapping sounds underwater.

Skink, Five-lined 11 in. *(27·9 cm.)*

Young FIVE-LINED SKINKS have blue tails, which become brownish as they grow older.

Skua 1½ ft. *(45·7 cm.)*

SKUAS are found in both the polar regions. In Antarctica they eat great numbers of Adélie penguin chicks.

Skunk, Striped 2 ft. *(60·9 cm.)*

The STRIPED SKUNK is well-known for the foul-smelling spray it uses in self-defence. It also helps many kinds of ducks by eating the eggs of snapping turtles. This controls the number of snappers, which eat young ducks.

Sloth, Two-toed 2 ft. 1 in. *(63·5 cm.)*

The TWO-TOED SLOTH has algae on its hair, giving it a greenish colour that may help it hide among the leaves of the trees it lives in. In zoos there is not enough light for the algae, and the sloth's real colours can be seen.

Slug 2 in. *(50·8 mm.)*

SLUGS are snails that have either no shell or a thin shell hidden under their outer skin.

Snail 1 to 4 in. *(25·4 to 101·6 mm.)*

SNAILS have a single large foot and a rasplike tongue that scrapes up bits of food. In dry weather they pull into their shells and seal off the opening.

Sidewinder Rattlesnake up to $2\frac{1}{2}$ ft. *(76·2 cm.)*

The SIDEWINDER RATTLESNAKE moves across the loose desert sand by an odd looping motion that leaves a series of slanting tracks instead of one continuous mark.

Snapper, Red 3 ft. *(91·4 cm.)*

One of the most sought-after food fishes is the RED SNAPPER, a deepwater fish that lives in the warmer parts of the sea.

Soft-shelled Turtle $1\frac{1}{2}$ ft. *(45·7 cm.)*

SOFT-SHELLED TURTLES make up for their lack of defensive armour by having fierce dispositions. In the water they look like swimming pancakes.

Sole 1 ft. *(30·4 cm.)*

SOLE are the smallest relatives of the halibut and flounder, and like them, they have heads twisted so that both eyes are on one side.

Sparrow, Chipping $5\frac{1}{2}$ in. *(13·9 cm.)*
The CHIPPING SPARROW has learned to live with man and is a common bird in suburbs.

Sparrow Hawk 1 ft. *(30·4 cm.)*
Although the SPARROW HAWK does eat sparrows and mice, it is particularly fond of insects and eats them whenever it can.

Sperm Whale 60 ft. *(18·2 m.)*
SPERM WHALES have been known to dive at least 3,000 ft. *(914 m.)* below the surface to catch giant squids. Man hunts them to the brink of extinction for their oil and meat; but there is no need to endanger these rare giants, because man-made substitutes are available for every product made from whales.

Spider, Garden up to 1 in. *(25·4 mm.)*
GARDEN SPIDERS spin their silken webs in places where flying insects are likely to be found.

Spider Monkey 1 ft. 10 in. *(55·8 cm.)*
The SPIDER MONKEY uses its long, grasping tail as an extra arm. It can hang by its tail and even pick things up with it.

Spoonbill, Roseate

2 ft. 10 in. *(86·3 cm.)*

ROSEATE SPOONBILLS slosh their flat bills through the mud in search of insects and crustaceans. Young spoonbills are white; it takes three years for their full colour to develop.

Springbok

4 ft. *(1·2 m.)*

The SPRINGBOK can jump 10 ft. *(3 m.)* into the air. Once one of the commonest antelope in South Africa, it is, after years of slaughter, now rare.

Squid, Giant

20 ft. *(6 m.)*

The GIANT SQUID, which can grow to be 50 ft. *(15 m.)* long, has a hard beak, like a parrot's. One of its chief enemies is the sperm whale; many of these whales carry scars from the squids' strong suckers.

Squirrel, Grey

1½ ft. *(45·7 cm.)*

The GREY SQUIRREL of eastern North America has been introduced into England and South Africa. It buries acorns and nuts in the autumn, and those it forgets to dig up again grow into new trees.

Squirrel Monkey

1 ft. 2 in. *(35·5 cm.)*

The SQUIRREL MONKEY is about the size and colour of a squirrel. It is commonly sold in pet shops to persons who don't know that because this monkey must live at a constant temperature of 70° or above, it is difficult to care for.

Stag Beetle 3 in. *(76·2 mm.)*

Male STAG BEETLES have large pincers that remind some persons of the antlers of a stag. Like deer, the males fight over females.

Starfish 6 in. *(15·2 cm.)*

Because STARFISH are one of the chief enemies of oysters, oyster growers used to catch them, cut them into pieces, and throw the pieces back into the sea—until they discovered that each piece grew into a new starfish.

Starling 8½ in. *(21·5 cm.)*

In the 1890's one hundred and twenty STARLINGS were taken to New York from England and set free. Today there are billions of starlings in America, all descended from the original birds.

Stilt, Black-necked 1 ft. 3 in. *(38·1 cm.)*

The BLACK-NECKED STILT's legs leave no doubt about where it got its name. Stilts wade in the water looking for food.

Stork, White 3 ft. 4 in. *(1 m.)*

In parts of Europe it is believed that a WHITE STORK nesting on a roof brings good luck to those in the house; in some villages people build platforms for the stork to make its nest on.

Sturgeon up to 10 ft. *(3 m.)*

STURGEONS are the largest freshwater fish. They have large bony plates on their skin instead of scales.

Sunfish, Ocean 6 ft. *(1·8 m.)*

The OCEAN SUNFISH is not related to the sunfish of fresh water. This giant is found in warm seas.

Swallow $7\frac{1}{2}$ in. *(19 cm.)*

The SWALLOW often sticks its mud and grass nest to a sheltered wall of a barn. It flies close to the surface of lakes and streams and catches low-flying insects.

Swallowtail

$3\frac{8}{10}$ in. *(96·5 mm.)* wingspan

SWALLOWTAILS are the largest butterflies found outside the tropics.

Swan $3\frac{1}{2}$ to 5 ft. *(1·1 to 1·5 m.)*

Because they cannot dive underwater, SWANS can feed only where the water is shallow enough to let them touch bottom with their bills. The MUTE SWAN has been domesticated for over eight hundred years, but has never become really tame. Much smaller is the BLACK-NECKED SWAN of southern South America.

Swift 5 in. *(12·7 cm.)*

SWIFTS fly with their mouths open in order to catch insects. They nest in cracks and holes in cliffs, trees and buildings.

Swordfish up to 15 ft. *(4·5 m.)*

SWORDFISH can stab their sharp swords through the bottom of a wooden boat. A big swordfish can weigh half a ton, though most are smaller.

Black-necked Swan

Mute Swan

Swallow

Swordfish

Swift

Tiger Swallowtail

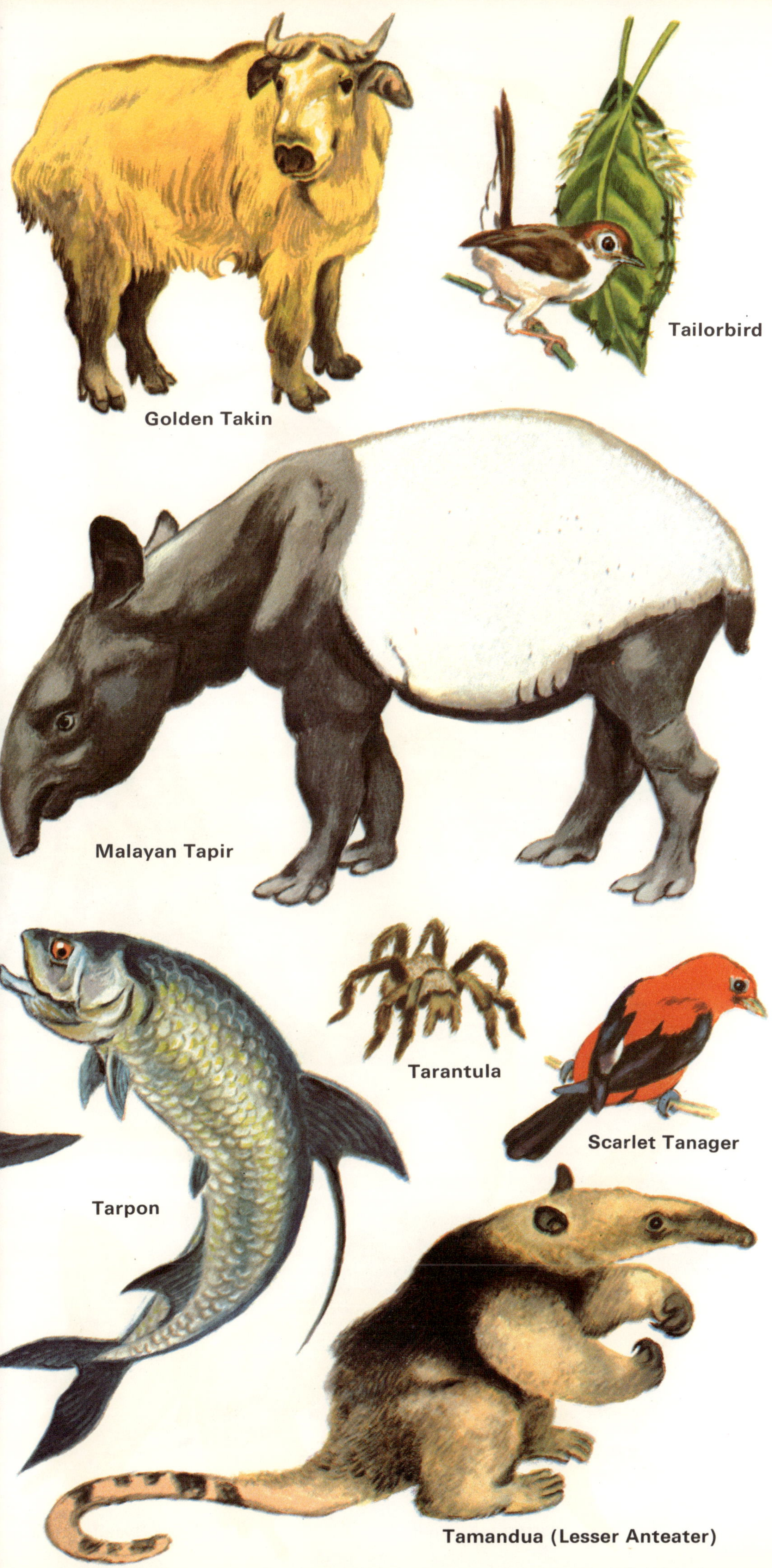

Golden Takin

Tailorbird

Malayan Tapir

Tarantula

Scarlet Tanager

Tarpon

Tamandua (Lesser Anteater)

Tailorbird 5 in. *(12·7 cm.)*

The TAILORBIRD protects its eggs by sewing leaves together with its bill, using strings of plant fibre or silk from cocoons as thread. The sewed leaves form a little tent.

Takin $3\frac{1}{2}$ ft. *(1·1 m.)*

The rare TAKIN, an expert climber, lives in high rhododendron forests in China and northern Burma. It has wavy hair.

Tamandua 2 ft. *(60·9 cm.)*

The TAMANDUA, like other anteaters, has no teeth, but defends itself from its enemies by slashing with its strong, sharp front claws.

Tanager, Scarlet 7 in. *(17·7 cm.)*

Only the male SCARLET TANAGER is red, and in the autumn he loses this colour in patches until he is greenish, like his mate.

Tapir, Malayan 7 ft. *(2·1 m.)*

The MALAYAN TAPIR seems to be wearing a white saddle. Baby tapirs are tan with whitish spots and streaks. Tapirs spend a lot of time in water, where they find tasty plants to eat.

Tarantula 7 in. *(17·7 cm.)* overall

TARANTULAS are the largest of all spiders. Some of the bigger ones eat small birds, but their bites are not dangerous to man.

Tarpon 4 ft. *(1·2 m.)*

The silvery TARPON can leap high out of the water. Because the tarpon is not very good to eat, most fishermen set it free after catching it.

Tarsier 6 in. *(15·2 cm.)*

TARSIERS have enormous eyes that help them find insects and small lizards in the dark. They leap nimbly from branch to branch like tiny acrobats.

Tasmanian Devil $2\frac{1}{2}$ ft. *(76·2 cm.)*

The TASMANIAN DEVIL raises its young in a pouch. It is not at all sociable and lives alone in a burrow.

Teal, Blue-winged 1 ft. 3 in. *(38·1 cm.)*

The BLUE-WINGED TEAL loses its wing feathers in summer and cannot fly again until late in the autumn. While it is flightless it replaces its bright body feathers with dull ones, making it difficult for an enemy to see.

Termite $\frac{3}{10}$ in. *(7·6 mm.)*

Some TERMITES live underground and some make large, hard nests in trees or on the ground. A few termites in each nest grow into "soldiers", which have big jaws and defend the rest of the termites from attack.

Tern 1 ft. 3 in. *(38·1 cm.)*

TERNS are small, streamlined cousins of the gulls. They nest in large colonies and live on small fishes they catch by diving from the air.

Terrapin, Diamondback 8 in. *(20·3 cm.)*

DIAMONDBACK TERRAPINS were once eaten in great quantities in the United States and have therefore become very rare.

Thrush, Wood 8 in. *(20·3 cm.)*

The WOOD THRUSH hunts for insects on the forest floor. Its flute-like song is one of the woodland's most beautiful sounds.

Tick $\frac{2}{10}$ in. *(5 mm.)*

TICKS have been known to live as long as five years without food. The WOOD TICK feeds on the blood of mammals and can carry disease.

Tiger up to 9 ft. *(2·7 m.)*

The TIGER is the largest of the cats, even larger than the lion. It is a forest animal, and because of hunters and the conversion of forests to farmland the tiger is becoming scarce. Only about three thousand tigers are alive in their wild state today.

Titmouse, Tufted 6 in. *(15·2 cm.)*

The perky TUFTED TITMOUSE can easily be tamed to light on a person's hand to take food.

Toad 4 in. *(101·6 mm.)*

TOADS can live in places too dry for frogs, but they must return to water in the spring to lay their eggs.

Toco Toucan 2 ft. 1 in. *(63·5 cm.)*

The TOCO TOUCAN's bright bill is filled with spongy bone, so that it is strong but very light. The bill is used to crush fruit.

Trout, Rainbow $1\frac{1}{2}$ ft. *(45·7 cm.)*

RAINBOW TROUT are one of America's favourite sport fishes. Fishermen catch them with "flies", fishhooks decorated with bits of feather or other material to make them look like insects.

Tuatara 2 ft. *(60·9 cm.)*

Although it looks like a lizard, the TUATARA is the last living reptile of a group that was common during the time of the dinosaurs.

Tuna 8 to 12 ft. *(2·4 to 3·6 m.)*
TUNA live in the open sea in schools. The BLUEFIN TUNA is the biggest—some weigh nearly a ton.

Turkey, Wild 4 ft. *(1·2 m.)*
If Benjamin Franklin had had his way, the WILD TURKEY, not the eagle, would have been the United States national bird. Although it flies quite well, the turkey prefers to escape its enemies by running.

Turtle, Snapping 1½ ft. *(45·7 cm.)*
The SNAPPING TURTLE often waits quietly underwater, keeping its greyish mouth open wide and wiggling a small, pink, wormlike flap on its tongue. Small fishes that come to eat the "worm" are snapped up by the turtle.

Uakari 2 ft. 1 in. *(63·5 cm.)*
The UAKARI is the only short-tailed monkey in the New World. The hair on top of its head is so short that it looks bald.

Umbrella Ant ⅜ in. *(7·6 mm.)*
UMBRELLA ANTS carry pieces of leaves above them like parasols. They take the leaves to their nests as food for a fungus they grow to eat.

Umbrella Bird 1 ft. 4 in. *(40·6 cm.)*
The UMBRELLA BIRD has a crest of feathers that it can spread forward to cover its head and most of its beak.

Urial 5 ft. *(1·5 m.)*
The URIAL is one of many kinds of wild sheep found throughout the mountains of the Northern Hemisphere.

Wild Turkey

Snapping Turtle

Uakari

Bluefin Tuna

Umbrella Bird

Urial

Umbrella Ant

Vampire Bat 3½ in. *(88·9 mm.)*

The VAMPIRE BAT makes a small, shallow cut in an animal's skin, then laps up the blood that oozes out, often without the victim's knowing it has been bitten. It lives entirely on blood.

Viceroy 3 in. *(76·2 mm.)* wingspan

Although the VICEROY does not taste bad to birds, they usually leave it alone because it looks so much like the monarch butterfly, which does taste bad.

Vicuña 5 ft. *(1·5 m.)*

The VICUÑA, a smaller cousin of the llama, has fine, long hair so useful to man that hunters and furriers have made the vicuña very scarce.

Viper, Horned 2 ft. *(60·9 cm.)*

The HORNED VIPER often buries itself in the desert sand during the heat of the day and seeks its food at night.

Vireo, White-eyed 6 in. *(15·2 cm.)*

The WHITE-EYED VIREO spends most of its time close to the ground. It hides its nest in the forest undergrowth a few feet above the ground.

Vole 4 in. *(101·6 mm.)*

VOLES are chunky, short-tailed mice. The BANK VOLE of Europe lives in a burrow in the woods.

Vulture 2 ft. 8 in. *(81·2 cm.)*

VULTURES live mainly on animals that are already dead. The KING VULTURE is the most brightly coloured of these bare-headed birds.

Walking Stick 3 in. *(76·2 mm.)*

WALKING STICKS bear little resemblance to their relatives the grasshoppers and the roaches. Some kinds grow to be over a foot long.

Wallaby 3 ft. *(91·4 cm.)*

WALLABIES, which are small kangaroos, act just like the big ones. They carry their babies in a pouch and are expert jumpers.

Walrus 12 ft. *(3·6 m.)*

The WALRUS uses its long tusks to dig clams from the floor of the sea.

Wapiti 8 ft. *(2·4 m.)*

The male WAPITI is not content with one mate and will fight with other males for possession of groups of females.

Warbler $5\frac{1}{2}$ in. *(13·9 cm.)*

In the autumn most WARBLERS are the same shade of yellow-green, but in the spring each kind has its own special colour pattern. The YELLOW-THROATED WARBLER nests high in the tops of tall trees.

Wasp, Paper $\frac{8}{10}$ in. *(20·3 mm.)*

The PAPER WASP does not build a large enclosed nest as some hornets do, but makes a flattened nest that is completely open on the underside.

Walking Stick

Red-necked Wallaby

Yellow-throated Warbler

Paper Wasp

Wapiti (American Elk)

Wart Hog 4½ ft. *(1·3 m.)*

The WART HOG holds its tail straight up when it runs. It prefers to shun danger, but when it has to fight, its sharp tusks make effective weapons.

Water Beetle 2 in. *(50·8 mm.)*

As adults, WATER BEETLES feed on dead creatures, but their young catch live prey for themselves.

Water Boatman ½ in. *(12·7 mm.)*

The WATER BOATMAN'S last pair of legs work like oars. With powerful kicks the boatman can dive deep in the water, but its body is so light that unless it clings to something it will bob back up to the surface.

Water Buffalo 9 ft. *(2·7 m.)*

A few wild WATER BUFFALO still exist, and there are many domesticated ones in Asia, where they are used as beasts of burden.

Water Bug, Giant

2½ to 4 in. *(63·5 to 101·6 mm.)*

The GIANT WATER BUG eats other water insects and even small fishes. It has a habit of flying around light bulbs and its bite is very painful.

Waxwing 8 in. *(20·3 cm.)*

The Waxwing lives in small flocks, except during nesting time late in the summer. It is one of the neatest-looking birds, with every feather sleeked down in place.

Weasel, Long-tailed $1\frac{1}{2}$ ft. *(45·7 cm.)*

In the northern parts of its range, the Long-tailed Weasel turns white in winter; elsewhere it is brown all year long.

Weevil, Boll $\frac{1}{3}$ in. *(8·3 mm.)*

The female Boll Weevil lays her eggs in the buds and bolls of the cotton plant, and the young weevils destroy the developing cotton.

Whale, Blue 100 ft. *(30·4 m.)*

Blue Whales, the biggest animals of any kind that ever lived, eat huge quantities of tiny sea creatures about the size of shrimp. They have been hunted almost to extinction, and the few that are still alive are in danger of being killed by whalers.

Whelk 3 to 4 in. *(76·2 to 101·6 mm.)*

WHELKS eat oysters, clams, and other molluscs that live in shallow water. They wait for a scallop to open its hinged double shell, then they wedge their own shell between them and eat the occupant.

Whippoorwill 10 in. *(25·4 cm.)*

Very few persons ever see a WHIPPOORWILL because it flies only after dark, but its call is a familiar sound on summer nights in the American countryside.

Whirligig Beetle $\frac{6}{10}$ in. *(15·2 mm.)*

The WHIRLIGIG BEETLE'S eyes are divided into upper and lower halves—half to see above the surface of the water and half to see below.

Whitefish, Lake 1 ft. 10 in. *(55·8 cm.)*

The LAKE WHITEFISH, like its relatives the trout, lives in cold waters. Because too many are being caught today, whitefish are no longer very numerous.

Whooping Crane 4 ft. 2 in. *(1·2 m.)*

Only a few dozen WHOOPING CRANES exist today. Each year they are counted, and their numbers are slowly increasing because the governments of the United States and Canada give them strict protection.

Wombat 3 ft. *(91·4 cm.)*

WOMBATS look less like their relatives the opossums and kangaroos than like overgrown woodchucks. Their habits are very much like those of woodchucks, and they eat the same kind of food.

Woodchuck 1 ft. 10 in. *(55·8 cm.)*

The WOODCHUCK is a very large squirrel that lives in burrows. It eats only plants and prefers to live alone.

Woodpecker 10 in. *(25·4 cm.)*

WOODPECKERS use their strong beaks to chisel into trees in search of insects. They have stiff tail feathers that help to prop them up as they bang away through the wood.

Woolly Monkey 2 ft. *(60·9 cm.)*

When the WOOLLY MONKEY is not using its tail to grasp a branch, it often curls up the tip.

Wrasse 2 ft. *(60·9 cm.)*

WRASSES have front teeth that stick out and rear teeth that are made for grinding hard shells. The flesh of wrasses that eat poisonous creatures becomes poisonous itself.

Wren 5 in. *(12·7 cm.)*

WRENS often build many nests in different places before deciding which one to move into.

Wolf, Timber 5 ft. *(1·5 m.)*

TIMBER WOLVES hunt together in packs and can sometimes catch even full-grown moose. Although they are persecuted by man, they actually help the moose and deer by keeping them from becoming too numerous for their food supply.

Wolverine 3 ft. *(91·4 cm.)*
The WOLVERINE has been known to break into trappers' cabins and ruin everything inside. It steals traps, eats animals killed by the traps, and is very clever at not being caught itself.

Yak $10\frac{1}{2}$ ft. *(3·2 m.)*, 7 ft. *(2·1 m.)* tall
The YAK'S long, shaggy coat protects it from the cold in its mountain home. Domesticated yaks can be trained to carry burdens; they provide food and milk, and their hair is used for wool.

Yapok 1 ft. *(30·4 cm.)*
The YAPOK is the only opossum that catches its food in the water. It has webbed feet and long, unwebbed fingers for feeling in the mud to find insects and other water creatures.

Yellow Jacket $\frac{8}{10}$ in. *(20·3 mm.)*
YELLOW JACKETS, a type of wasp, nest under or above the ground. They are quick to sting anyone who disturbs their nest.

Yucca Moth $\frac{3}{10}$ in. *(7·6 mm.)*
The YUCCA MOTH and yucca plant of America have evolved together. The yucca moth is the only insect that can pollinate the yucca flowers, and while its young eat yucca seeds, they never eat too many on one plant. In this way the moth and plant ensure each other's survival.

Zebra 7 ft. *(2·1 m.)*
ZEBRAS are small wild horses. The lion was their chief enemy until man came along and proved to be a worse one.

Zorille 1 ft. 1 in. *(33 cm.)*
The ZORILLE, which lives in Africa and is a close relative of the skunk, looks like a small skunk and can give off a foul-smelling scent.

Index

NOTE: **Boldface** type indicates pages on which illustrations appear.

D

E

F

G

N

O

P

Q

R

Y

Z